MASTERS AT WORK

Becoming a Sommelier

Becoming a Curator

Becoming an Architect

Becoming a Fashion Designer

Becoming a Sports Agent

Becoming an Interior Designer

Becoming a Firefighter

Becoming a Nurse

Becoming a Video Game Designer

Becoming a Midwife

Becoming a Teacher

MASTERS AT WORK

BECOMING A SPORTS AGENT

GARY RIVLIN

SIMON & SCHUSTER

New York   London   Toronto   Sydney   New Delhi

Simon & Schuster
1230 Avenue of the Americas
New York, NY 10020

First Simon & Schuster hardcover edition February 2021

SIMON & SCHUSTER and colophon are registered trademarks of Simon & Schuster, Inc.

For information about special discounts for bulk purchases, please contact
Simon & Schuster Special Sales at 1-866-506-1949 or business@simonandschuster.com.

The Simon & Schuster Speakers Bureau can bring authors to your live event.
For more information or to book an event, contact the Simon & Schuster Speakers Bureau
at 1-866-248-3049 or visit our website at www.simonspeakers.com.

Illustrations by Donna Mehalko © 2021

Manufactured in the United States of America

3 5 7 9 10 8 6 4 2

Library of Congress Cataloging-in-Publication Data

Names: Rivlin, Gary, author.
Title: Becoming a sports agent / Gary Rivlin.
Description: First Simon & Schuster hardcover edition. |
New York : Simon & Schuster, 2021. | Series: Masters at work |
Includes bibliographical references.
Identifiers: LCCN 2020032865 (print) | LCCN 2020032866 (ebook) |
ISBN 9781501167973 (hardcover) | ISBN 9781501167980 (ebook)
Subjects: LCSH: Sports agents--United States. | Sports agents--Vocational guidance--United States.
Classification: LCC GV734.5 .R58 2021 (print) | LCC GV734.5 (ebook) |
DDC 796.04/4068--dc23
LC record available at https://lccn.loc.gov/2020032865
LC ebook record available at https://lccn.loc.gov/2020032866

ISBN 978-1-5011-6797-3
ISBN 978-1-5011-6798-0 (ebook)

To Daisy, Oliver, and Silas

CONTENTS

BECOMING A
SPORTS AGENT

INTRODUCTION

NFL agent Tory Dandy stepped onto the field under an overcast sky. He wore the sports agent's uniform: untucked dress shirt, jeans, and sneakers. In a few hours, the New York Jets would host the Cleveland Browns at MetLife Stadium in New Jersey, across the river from Manhattan. Dandy, a fit thirty-nine-year-old black man, scanned the field. Three of the thirty-five NFL players he represented were there, warming up for that night's game. He took a deep breath and steeled himself for the evening ahead.

Though it was only two weeks into the 2019 NFL season, Dandy had already flown more flights than most of us log in a year. He was exhausted and sick. "Living the dream," he said sarcastically.

Dandy had gone over his itinerary on the ride from his hotel in midtown Manhattan to the stadium. He spent

Labor Day at home in Charlotte, North Carolina, but the next day was on a plane to Minneapolis, where a veteran player, unhappy with his current agent, had asked for a meeting. From there it was a short flight to Chicago to see one client's season opener, a Thursday night game pitting the Bears against the Green Bay Packers, and then a longer one to Tampa Bay to see another client's opener that Sunday. The following Monday he flew to New Orleans to see the Saints play the Houston Texans—"I had five guys playing in that game," he said—and then to Boston, where he met another veteran unhappy with his representation. After a couple of days back in Charlotte, Dandy was on a flight to New York on Saturday morning to kick off a kind of football double-header: the Giants were playing the Buffalo Bills that Sunday at MetLife, and the Jets were hosting the Browns the next day at the same stadium.

Dandy had felt a tickle in his throat on Saturday morning. By the time the Uber driver dropped him off at the New Jersey home of a rookie linebacker for the Giants named Oshane Ximines, Dandy's throat was raw and his body ached. But clients play through pain, and so he would do the same. There was lunch with a Giants veteran he had only recently taken on as a client and then two more meetings, one at the home of a third member of the Giants and another at the Jersey City hotel where the Bills were staying. It wasn't until after 9:00 p.m. that he got back to his hotel room, where he chugged some throat medicine and collapsed. He still had two games to attend and get-togethers with the two Jets and one Brown he represented who were playing on *Monday Night Football*.

There were moments, Dandy confessed, when he dreamed of taking the next plane home—but then he did what might be called agent math. Dandy meets face-to-face with each of his clients at least once during the season. Forget how it would look to his clients; going home early would mean makeup trips that would spill into the second half of the season—and November and December were generally reserved for visiting with the families of college players he hoped to sign after the end of the NCAA season. Signing two or three promising draftees each year is essential to a thriving practice, especially in a league where the average pro career lasts 3.3 years. "Recruiting is a never-ending part of my life," Dandy said.

And, apparently, a never-ending headache.

We were just past the worst of the Holland Tunnel traffic when Dandy's phone rang. It was Jimmy Sexton, a senior partner at Creative Artists Agency (CAA), the talent-agency behemoth that has employed Dandy since 2016. Sexton is a legend in the industry, a large, loud-talking southern deal-maker whose client list includes Julio Jones, once the league's best wide receiver, and Philip Rivers, sixth on the NFL's all-time career passing touchdown leaders list. Sexton was calling from Memphis to talk about a promising collegian both he and Dandy thought would be signing with CAA at the end of the season (NCAA rules dictate that a player can't commit to an agent until after his or her final game). Now the player and his family were ghosting them. Sexton, who speaks in a booming, swampy voice, was phoning Dandy with the latest. Apparently, the family had hired a lawyer.

"Getting a lawyer without letting me know! There's definitely some bullshit going on," Sexton bellowed. Dandy had more bad news for his colleague: he had looked at the recruit's Twitter account. The player was following Drew Rosenhaus and David Mulugheta, two of the NFL's higher-profile agents. Sexton repeated himself: "Definitely some bullshit going on." Dandy promised he would find out what he could and hung up just before we reached the stadium.

Dandy had been at MetLife the day before, and between

hacking coughs and slugs of water, he guided the Uber driver to the drop-off point. After checking in with security, we walked through a tunnel and onto the field. Kickoff was more than two hours away, but already the sidelines were thick with photographers. Odell Beckham Jr., a star on the Giants until he was traded to the Browns during the off-season, was making his first appearance in the stadium that had been his home for the previous five years, and they were there to capture the moment. Already there were fans in the stands holding up signs that were critical of Beckham, who was warming up on the field, a broad smile on his face. Adding to the sizzle of that night's game was that these were the new-and-improved Browns. Beckham, one of the NFL's more electrifying receivers, was being paired with Baker Mayfield, the number-one pick in the 2018 draft. The Browns also had the number-four pick in 2018, which they used to choose defensive standout Denzel Ward, whom Dandy represented. Ward, a cornerback, wasn't nearly as high-profile a player as either Beckham or Mayfield, but he had made the Pro Bowl as a rookie. Ward was in the second year of a four-year, $29 million contract that Dandy negotiated. A big game on national TV would give Dandy another talking point when he was ready to haggle over Ward's next deal.

Players for both teams were warming up in shorts, T-shirts, and sweatshirts. Dandy spotted Ward loosening up with some of his teammates and called out to him. "Denzel!" he tried yelling between coughs. "Denzel!" He waved an arm. Ward finally noticed him and jogged over. Agent and player clasped hands and tapped shoulders in a bro hug. Dandy then whispered into Ward's ear some "words of encouragement." He said more or less the same to each of his players that night, he told me, whether they'd had a great first week or a poor one.

Jamison Crowder, a veteran wide receiver whom the Jets had signed during the off-season, had a stellar debut, catching fourteen passes for ninety-nine yards. "This is your chance," Dandy reminded him during their bro-hug, "to make an indelible impression in front of a national audience."

Robby Anderson, another Jets receiver, was also a client. Anderson was an undrafted walk-on from Temple University who, since he joined the team in 2016, had proven to be one of the Jets' more reliable wideouts. Yet Anderson had played so poorly in the opener that his head coach publicly criticized his play. A few days earlier, the team traded for another receiver, a former Pro Bowler whom the blogs cast as a threat to Anderson's playing time.

"I told Robby, just like I told my other guys, 'This is a prime-time game. *Monday Night Football*. Against the Browns. Odell's first trip back to New York. A lot of media attention, a lot of people watching,'" Dandy said. "I told him he has a big opportunity in front of him that could make everyone forget last week." Anderson certainly had the talent. During warm-ups, he was making showy one-handed grabs and even caught a punted ball behind his back. To see any of these players up close—even one who's worried about his future with the team—is to realize how extraordinarily athletic each of them is.

While Dandy was still on the Browns' side of the field, an earnest young man in his early thirties walked over and shook his hand. It was Chris Cooper, the Browns' vice president of football administration—the team's "cap guy." These days, every NFL team has at least one person whose job it is to monitor player salaries so the team doesn't go over the strict limit the NFL imposes ($188.2 million in 2019). A team that exceeds that amount can pay a fine of $5 million and risk losing a draft choice. The "cap guy" is essential to running a modern-day franchise, and is often Dandy's first point of contact when negotiating a deal—the person who understands how much an organization can afford given the salaries of all the other players they have under contract. For Cleveland, that was Cooper.

"He's always beating me," Cooper said of Dandy. But then, canned compliments come free. It's the more tangible concessions—such as an extra option year or an additional few hundred thousand dollars in incentives—that are harder to extract.

Nick Sabella, a carbon copy of Cooper, was our escort once Dandy was ready to visit the Jets' side of the field. Sabella, who graduated from Tulane Law in 2012 as opposed to Cooper's matriculation at Brooklyn Law School, had gone to work for the Jets' front office in 2019, after nearly six years with the Bears. Sabella was dressed almost exactly like Cooper, except that he wore a green tie (the Jets' color) to match his dark suit rather than an orange one (the Browns' color), and Sabella's short brown hair was curly rather than straight. The Jets had gone into their locker room to change into their uniforms at that point, so Dandy staked out a spot by the players' tunnel, popping cough drops and chatting with Sabella.

When the Jets exited their locker room, they were dressed in black uniforms with green trim. Close-up, and with their helmets on, they looked like stormtroopers ready for battle, especially those wearing tinted visors. Jamison Crowder spotted Dandy and ran over for his bro-hug and pep talk before rejoining his fellow receivers. That prompted a bit of reminiscing between Dandy and Sabella. The two of them seemed to have set some kind of record when agreeing to the three-year, $28.5 million deal that Dandy had negotiated for Crowder earlier in the year. "I was very up-front with Tory about Crowder," Sabella said. "I told him, 'We like him a lot; we're coming hard at him.' Tory was equally direct with me." Crowder had been with the Washington Redskins for four years, but a few hours after the start of the 2019 free-agency period, he was a member of the Jets. "We had a deal within thirty minutes," Sabella said.

Among the perks of working for CAA is an internal ticket broker who invariably has Dandy sitting more or less at the fifty-yard line, and never far from the field. We took our seats, and immediately Dandy was back on his phone. A few minutes into the first quarter, he took out the backup power pack he had slipped into his pocket before leaving the hotel. "When my guys call, I pick up," he said.

The seats were great, but that only meant a better vantage point for enduring what might have been the worst professional football game I've ever seen. The Jets' starting quarterback, Sam Darnold, was out with mono, and New York's backup had thrown for all of three yards before badly injuring his ankle on a late hit midway through the second quarter. Somehow, Robby Anderson managed to shine, notching eighty-one yards on four catches. But he was the lone bright spot during an otherwise dismal game for the Jets, who would start the season with back-to-back home losses.

Odell Beckham Jr., on the other hand, was sensational. Five minutes into the game, he lit up the crowd with an incredible one-handed grab (his specialty) that led to the Browns' first score. Beckham put the game away near the end of the third quarter with a ten-yard slant over the middle that he turned into an eighty-nine-yard touchdown catch. "His first time back in New York and on the big stage, he put on a show," Dandy said. For a moment, the fan in Dandy peeked out from behind his all-business facade. "That's football, man."

In the Uber back to his hotel, Dandy slumped in a corner of the back seat, popped another cough drop, took yet another sip of water, and made a crack about the supposedly glamorous life of an NFL agent. He brought up a question I had asked him earlier in the evening, before it looked like he ought to have been hooked up to an intravenous drip: What's the downside of being a big-time agent? "This!" he said plaintively.

Is THERE A PROFESSION more alluring than that of sports agent, and a job more repellent? On the one hand, the "athlete agent," to use the legal term for the profession, is confidant and friend to the adored and famous. There's glory in making a living—often a very good living—in professional sports and in the thrill that comes from proximity to celebrity. The agent is an insider who shares a client's successes without the pressures of having to perform in big games and the risks of injury or high-profile humiliation.

Yet an agent is sometimes nothing more than a glorified personal assistant. Rafa Nieves is vice president of baseball at Wasserman, which, like CAA, is another giant of the sports agent world. His clients include a long list of major leaguers, including Chicago White Sox closer Alex Colomé, whom Nieves met when he was just starting out and was paid $1,000 as a "runner" for every promising minor leaguer he signed. Nieves has negotiated nearly $25 million in contracts on Colomé's behalf, generating well over $1 million in fees for his agency. "If Alex Colomé calls and asks, 'Can you make a reservation for me and my wife?' or an appointment with a pediatrician, I can't tell him, 'Call Yvonne in my office.' I'm doing that myself," Nieves said.

The job does bring incredible perks, starting with the best tickets to any game—Super Bowls and World Series included—and first-class airline tickets. But with those perks come the miserable moments born of a job that entails too much travel. The first time I met Tory Dandy was about a month before the start of the 2019 NFL season, when he was in New Jersey to sign a Giants veteran who had been looking to switch agents. So torrential was the rain that afternoon and evening that Dandy's flight, along with most others out of Newark Liberty International Airport, had been canceled. He was stuck for the night in New Jersey, six hundred miles from home, without a change of clothes or even a toothbrush. When I visited Rafa Nieves in Los Angeles, he pulled out his phone to show me his American Airlines account. It was the middle of September, and he had already flown eighty-three thousand miles with that one airline. He estimated he had flown another fifteen or twenty thousand miles on others. Almost every agent I spoke with had stories of multiple trips to far-flung towns to meet with prospects and their families, only to learn that those players had chosen someone else.

Agents are objects of envy. They're also objects of scorn. Fairly or unfairly, fans blame them for the huge salaries that translate into ticket prices so high that a family of four practically has to take out a home equity loan to enjoy a day at the ballpark. And few professions are more competitive. The agents you'll meet in these pages—most of them, at least— prove that it's possible to remain ethical and still make it to the top. But all of them have encountered dishonest and dishonorable competitors, if not scoundrels willing to do practically anything to pry away a client. To gain advantage, competitors have bad-mouthed them with made-up stories. They've lured away clients by dangling keys to an SUV parked out front that could be theirs just by signing. That raises another downside of calling oneself a sports agent: guilt by association.

Baseball people mention Ron Shapiro first or second when asked about agents who have honorably plied the trade. Over a career that has spanned four decades, Shapiro has represented Hall of Famers Cal Ripken Jr., Kirby Puckett, and Brooks Robinson, and even coauthored a book called *The Power of Nice*. And yet, Shapiro said, "My whole career I've been fighting this idea that agents are sleazeballs, just these slick quick-buck artists in it only for themselves. Being an agent means living with that."

There are too many agents, no matter the sport. Maybe a few dozen agents were working with baseball players back when Shapiro started out. These days, baseball has more than four hundred registered agents, and football has twice that many. A maximum of 224 players are selected in each NFL draft, and invariably successful agents represent multiple collegians each year. There were precisely eight hundred agents registered with the NFL Players Association in 2019. The math dictates that the vast majority won't represent anyone in a given draft. Some, no doubt, go multiple years in a row without picking up a client. In the public imagination, agents are intimate with big-name stars. In reality, most represent players few of us know, if they represent anyone at all.

A movie—*Jerry Maguire*—is one reason there are so many agents. The fictitious character of Jerry Maguire, along with others such as Arliss Michaels that followed, helped plant the idea of becoming an agent in the minds of many fans. But it's the money—specifically television money—that is a better explanation for the glut. Sports franchises have many revenue streams: ticket sales, concessions, licensing and merchandising, and corporate sponsorships. But no matter the sport, the biggest moneymaker is broadcasting rights. Television accounts for around half the dollars a given league generates each year. That figure is closer to 60 percent for football.

In the mid-1970s, a football team's share of the league's television contracts was approximately $2.4 million a year. In 2018, the league's thirty-two franchises received more than one hundred times that: nearly $255 million each in television revenue, based on the almost $8 billion that CBS, Fox, ESPN, DirectTV, and other media outlets pay annually for the rights to broadcast NFL games. Player salaries—and, by extension, the commissions agents collect when negotiating contracts—have grown accordingly. The average salary of an NFL player in the mid-1970s was under $60,000. In 2018, the average was $2.8 million. That works out to an annual fee of $84,000, and of course the top-tier agents represent a few dozen clients at once, if not more.

There are two basic financial arrangements for agents. Tory Dandy and Rafa Nieves work for larger agencies and are salaried employees, but their earnings each year are tied directly to the contracts they negotiate on behalf of their clients. A certified agent working for a large outfit earns a base salary of maybe $100,000 a year. "The money is all in the commissions," Nieves said, adding, "A partner at one of the big agencies who has everything working can end up making between two million and five million a year." Most, however, earn nowhere near that. Plenty break into the field, Nieves said, and leave within several years either because they don't like the job or because their take-home pay doesn't justify the stress and the lifestyle.

Other agents are independent and work for themselves or with a partner. Their earning power, as superagent Scott Boras has demonstrated over several decades, is nearly limitless. Boras is a former baseball player who never made it past Double-A yet brings in as much as the game's highest-paid stars. In just the first few days of baseball's 2019 free-agency period, he negotiated nearly $900 million worth of contracts, including a record-setting $324 million deal on behalf of pitcher Gerrit Cole. In less than a week, he had earned roughly $44 million in fees. And that doesn't include the commissions that Boras, who has an estimated net worth of $450 million, pockets for the commercials, endorsements, and other deals that he and his people negotiate on behalf of the players his agency—immodestly called the Boras Corporation—represents. Major League Baseball places a 5 percent cap on the fee an agent can collect when negotiating a contract, compared to 4 percent in the NBA and 3 percent in the NFL. There is no cap, however, on an agent's cut of a marketing deal. A local car dealer might offer a player between $20,000 and $30,000 (plus use of a car) for an endorsement. A regional dealer might pay a major player $200,000. A TV commercial on behalf of a car maker could be worth as much as $1 million. "A lot of the time we're making more on the marketing than on the contract," said Matt Sosnick, cofounder of Sosnick Cobbe & Karon, one of baseball's more successful independent agencies. Agents charge a fee of as much as 25 percent on marketing deals.

"We charge fifteen percent because we do such a high volume of these deals [that] we have no reason to charge more," said Sosnick, whose client list includes Pete Alonso, the rookie sensation whose fifty-three home runs during the 2019 season set the all-time record for a first-year player. One season into Alonso's career, Sosnick's agency had earned approximately $73,000 in commissions on his contract with the Mets but "way more than that" on his endorsements and sponsorship deals. (Sosnick would be arrested on domestic violence and child endangerment charges at the end of 2019.)

And yet, as Sosnick and others point out, earning a living

isn't easy even when an agent represents multiple clients. A baseball agent, for instance, typically picks up the costs of bats, gloves, and cleats for clients working their way through the minors. Soft touches like Sosnick also occasionally buy groceries on behalf of minor leaguers living off a salary of maybe $1,000 or $2,000 a month during the season.

"Factoring in equipment and travel, you're spending three thousand dollars per player per year, and that doesn't account for your time," Sosnick said. "You've got guys who stick around for five years in the minors; that's all your time plus fifteen grand." His first fourteen clients, Sosnick said, failed to make it to the majors, and the fifteenth pitched all of twelve innings in the bigs. "If you've picked the wrong guy, you get no return," he said. "And when you're a guy like I used to be and [are] just starting out, you can only choose wrong guys, because the best guys are going to choose agents with more experience." Ten years passed before Sosnick started making any money as an agent. It took another few years before he started making the kind of profits that justified his efforts.

The economics of football are similarly challenging. An NFL agent who signs a potential draftee is expected to get that prospect ready for football's scouting combine, held each year in Indianapolis at the end of February. The stakes are enormous; teams send coaches, scouts, and others to evaluate the three hundred collegians who are invited to audition for the NFL. Each prospect is put through a battery of strength, speed, agility, and mental tests. A poor showing in any category can be costly, just as cutting a tenth of a second off a prospect's time in the forty-yard dash is potentially worth millions of dollars. To get an athlete ready for the combine, a football agent typically spends at least $20,000 on trainers and training facilities.

"You're paying for housing during training, you're paying for advanced nutrition, and potentially a car rental," said famed football agent Leigh Steinberg, who has represented ten Hall of Famers over a career that has spanned more than four decades. It's the agent who typically pays to send players to the college all-star games that will showcase their talents and who picks up the costs of any private auditions and workouts that teams request. Most agents, Steinberg said, give a new signee a per diem because they're no longer on scholarship, and there are also out-of-pocket travel costs. Yet a player chosen in the fifth or sixth round, say, will get a signing bonus of maybe $75,000, earning an agent just over $2,000 in fees.

"You've spent thirty, thirty-five thousand dollars on this player, you collect twenty-one hundred on the signing bonus, and then maybe your player makes the team, but maybe he doesn't," Steinberg said. The first-rounders sign enormous contracts in the tens of millions of dollars. Teams have to pay a premium to sign a second- or third-round pick. But later draft choices typically earn the league minimum of $495,000. Then the agent's fee works out to just under $15,000 for that one season, which has to cover travel and any other expenses incurred while stage-managing a new player's introduction to the NFL. (The bigger agencies cover agents' travel costs.)

Heartbreak is part of the business. So is betrayal. Being an agent means operating in a marketplace that can be as cold as it is cruel. Consider the baseball agent who has invested $15,000 or more in a young baseball prospect and, not incidentally, has gotten emotionally involved in that player's life. The client starts to feel like family as he works his way through the development leagues and the tiered farm system (Single-A, Double-A, and Triple-A) that every major league team uses to nurture young talent. Then that player, just before the big signing that would have made it all worth it, lets you know (possibly via text) that, after all these years, he's leaving you for a bigger, better-known rival.

"You will likely have someone steal your client," said Bob Boland, who represented ten NFL players before becoming a part-time agent in 2000 to help NYU create its sports management program. "You will steal someone else's client. Those are two constants of working as a sports agent." Leigh Steinberg feels fortunate that only a few clients have dropped him for a rival. But he's suffered what is maybe an even worse betrayal—twice, which is the number of times a young acolyte of Steinberg's took clients of his to open a rival shop. In the first instance, the young lawyer Steinberg had taken under his wing struck when he knew his boss would be away on his honeymoon in Hawaii.

"You could say that being an agent isn't the most congenial of professions," Steinberg offered in obvious understatement. He then added, "One of the unfortunate things about our industry is that people who show bad behavior often end up the winners."

And yet, despite everything—despite the lack of congeniality and a hypercompetitive environment that inevitably means multiple broken hearts over a career—the agents featured here can't imagine making a living any other way. There's no doubt that it can be a demanding, sometimes disheartening profession, but it can also be rewarding. "You have an opportunity to help another human being reach his dreams, and that's a really great feeling," said Don Yee, who represents quarterback Tom Brady, among other clients. "I think most credible agents feel this way." Negatives notwithstanding, Tory Dandy described himself as "blessed" to be an NFL agent. So, too, did Leigh Steinberg. Those who have braved the field and made it tend to feel as if they've won the lottery.

A soccer agent named Jonathan Barnett topped *Forbes* magazine's 2019 list of the world's most powerful agents with $1.3 billion under contract, with expected commissions of $128 million. (Soccer agents are permitted to take as much as 10 percent of a player's contract.) Two more agents representing soccer players rank in the top five. There's big money to be made in other sports, too, including hockey, tennis, and golf, the sport that produced the original modern-day agent. Agents can also make a handsome living representing coaches, assistant coaches, retired Olympians, auto racers, and gamers who excel at virtual competitions.

Yet a quartet of football agents—Steinberg and Dandy, along with Don Yee and Drew Rosenhaus, who happily fills the bad-guy role as the agent who will do anything to succeed— are the primary focus of these pages. That decision wasn't born out of some great preference for football but was based on more practical matters: I didn't want to bog things down with the minutiae of each sport.

Being an agent is being an agent: recruiting players, negotiating contracts, fishing for endorsements and sponsorship deals, and doing what those in the business call "client maintenance," which basically means that if a player calls at 2:00 a.m., their agent answers the phone. Every sport, however, has its own rules and practices, its own unique dynamics. Baseball agents recruit players while they're still in high school, while those concentrating on football or basketball sell their services to collegians just before they're ready to go pro. The NBA draft lasts two rounds and involves sixty players; in contrast, more than one thousand baseball prospects are chosen during baseball's draft, which lasts at least forty rounds. Salaries are guaranteed in baseball and basketball but not in football, where the only money that's certain is the signing bonus. In the NFL, a player is typically paid only so long as a team chooses to keep him on the roster. The salaries are generally lower in the NFL than they are in baseball, which has no salary cap, or in basketball, which has a soft cap. Among the work-arounds in the NBA is the concept of "max contract" players, which is the league's way of discounting the enormous salaries earned by its highest-paid stars. Baseball and basketball (but not football) have a "luxury tax," and every sport seems to have its own mind-numbing formula for calculating team payrolls. During my initial conversation with Tory Dandy, the first agent I met with face-to-face, he mentioned "dead cap" money and also explained the differences among "signing bonuses," "roster bonuses," "option bonuses," and "restructuring bonuses." It was then that I realized I needed to focus on a single sport.

Dandy is the least-known and youngest of the four agents featured here, but he's a rising star. He represented a top-five pick in both the 2018 and 2019 drafts, which was a nice follow-up to 2017, when he represented three players taken among the first thirteen drafted. Steinberg, who started in the business in 1975, is one of the greats of the industry: the real-life Jerry Maguire (filmmaker Cameron Crowe shadowed Steinberg while researching the movie) and also an innovator who helped define what it means to be a modern sports agent. His client list over the years has included quarterbacks Warren Moon, Steve Young, and Troy Aikman, and also Bruce Smith, the league's all-time sacks leader, and Eric Dickerson, who still holds the record for most rushing yards in a season. Steinberg suffered what he described as "my fall" at the start of the 2000s but, at age sixty-five, this man for whom the term "superagent" had been practically invented started over, relearning the craft he had mastered in an earlier era. Yee started thirteen years after Steinberg, in 1987, and Rosenhaus signed his first client in 1989, when he was twenty-two years old and still in law school.

There's more than one way to become an agent, as the mentors you'll meet here will show, and more than one approach to the job. Steinberg is a glad-hander and schmoozer famous for the bash he throws at the Super Bowl each year. Rosenhaus has a similarly oversize personality that has him boasting of late nights at clubs with bottle service, wooing new talent and carousing with his famous clients. Both are shameless braggarts in a profession in which the client the prototypical agent most ardently represents is himself. Dandy and Yee are more modest, unassuming figures, yet there's no doubting Dandy's success, nor Yee's: besides Brady, he represents Patriots star Julian Edelman, along with Jimmy Garoppolo, the starting quarterback for the San Francisco 49ers, and Sean Payton, the longtime head coach of the Saints.

Yee is unusual, too, in that he rarely attends regular-season games to see one of his players. "I'm not judging others that do it that way," he said. "That's their formula. That's just not my formula." For most football agents, the combine in Indianapolis at the end of February is a fixture on the calendar, on par with Thanksgiving or Easter. In thirty-plus years in the business, Yee told me, he's been to the combine maybe three times, and then only because that's where the league started holding mandatory agent seminars. Similarly, he's a no-show at the Pro Bowl in Orlando at the end of the football season, and at the various college all-star games. Other agents attend those games, if only to fend off advances by rivals seeking to lure away their best players. "I was unstoppable at the All-Star games, such as the Blue-Grey game, the Senior Bowl, the Hula Bowl, and the East-West Shrine Game," boasted Drew Rosenhaus, an agent reviled by peers for his success in poaching players from them.

"If Drew didn't exist, we'd have to create him," Leigh Steinberg said when I visited him at his waterfront office in Newport Beach, California. "Because there are clients who are going to want the things that I offer, like role modeling and second careers and a quiet way of negotiating, and others who want an agent driving for every last dollar to be the whole mantra." Steinberg brought up Rosenhaus's best-known client, Antonio Brown, who a few weeks earlier had managed to wipe out $29.1 million in "guaranteed" money when his threats and other antics prompted the Oakland (now Las Vegas) Raiders to drop him before the start of his first season with the team.

Steinberg expressed a begrudging respect for Rosenhaus, whom he described as "smart and obviously very successful." But evidently Brown needed someone to help counsel and guide him, or at least to provide a release valve before he took to Twitter to destroy his career. "The job is about more than getting the biggest contract you can," Steinberg said.

1

Once He Was King

Gone is most of the memorabilia: the autographed footballs and jerseys from Warren Moon, Troy Aikman, and Steve Young. Lost, too, are the framed photos of a grinning Leigh Steinberg next to the big-name athletes he's represented over the years: Ricky Williams, Ben Roethlisberger, Thurman Thomas, Eric Dickerson, Earl Campbell. There were shots, too, of him with Tom Cruise and Cuba Gooding Jr. on the set of *Jerry Maguire*. But he put everything in storage when his life crashed and he was evicted from his high-rent offices in Newport Beach's Fashion Island. By the time he declared bankruptcy in 2012, he was more than $3 million in debt.

"They took my storage lockers, and one of the creditors cleaned me out," Steinberg said. He motioned to the walls in his new, less majestic office. There's a picture of him with Barack Obama, and another with Julia Roberts. A framed Aikman jersey he managed to hold on to hangs on one wall, and a pair of boxing gloves signed by Lennox Lewis sits under glass on a coffee table. Mostly, the office is an homage to one client, Kansas City Chiefs quarterback Patrick Mahomes II, who people were already speculating might become the NFL's first $200 million player (generating $6 million in fees for Steinberg Sports & Entertainment). I had to shift my eyes as we spoke so that I wasn't staring at Mahomes, whose picture hung over Steinberg's shoulder. There were Kansas City keepsakes and framed magazine covers featuring Mahomes scattered around the office, but most striking was a series of photos on the wall behind Steinberg's desk: blowups of pictures taken when Mahomes, a cell phone cradled to his ear, learned that the Chiefs had made him the number-ten pick in the 2017 draft. There's a look of ecstatic relief on the quarterback's face, but it's Steinberg, sitting just to the left of his client, who is more openly celebrating his providence. In one shot, Steinberg is pumping his fist; in another, his fists are raised triumphantly above his head. He was back on top.

Steinberg had just seen Mahomes a few days earlier in Oakland, where the young quarterback threw for 443 yards and four touchdowns in an easy win over the Raiders. That Sunday he was heading to Kansas City to see the Chiefs host the Baltimore Ravens. Steinberg was dressed in beat-up cargo shorts, running shoes, and a red T-shirt under a striped dress shirt that he left untucked. His once boyish face was bloated and red, his sandy hair unkempt. The thick wad of tobacco under his lip had him spitting into a cup for much of our time together. He leaned back in his chair, propped a foot against his desk, and, not for the first time, told me about his glory days, including the ten Hall of Famers he represented.

"I've had sixty-two first-round picks," he said. "The very first pick overall eight times. Some weekends I was representing half the starting quarterbacks in football." He had built one of the most impressive sports-agent practices in history and then watched it collapse, and now was building it back. "Living in your parents' house," he said, "having no more clients, drinking a bottle of vodka every day—that tends to put things in perspective."

STEINBERG THOUGHT HE MIGHT work in politics, or try his hand at acting, in which he dabbled as an undergraduate at the University of California, Berkeley. Or work as a news reporter or assistant district attorney. It was 1975, and the truth was that Steinberg, who'd stayed at Berkeley to earn a law degree, had no idea what he wanted to do. Then his friend Steve Bartkowski invited him to dinner. Steinberg's father was a high school teacher turned principal, his mother a librarian. He had grown up comfortably in Los Angeles, but his family was hardly rich. To help pay for law school, Steinberg worked as a dorm counselor. By chance, he was assigned to a dorm housing some of the school's football players, including Bartkowski, then the team's backup quarterback. The two had become friends long before Bartkowski, whom Steinberg calls Bart, was the number-one pick in the 1975 NFL draft. The Cal coach had sent Bartkowski to the same lawyer who had negotiated contracts on behalf of previous Cal stars, but talks with the Atlanta Falcons, the team that had drafted him first overall, were stalled. Over dinner, Bart asked his friend if he could take over.

There was no template for being an agent in the mid-1970s. It was barely a profession. Babe Ruth famously used a Boston druggist to represent him in salary negotiations. When one of Vince Lombardi's star players, future Hall of Famer Jim Ringo, showed up with an agent to a meeting with the legendary coach and general manager, Lombardi supposedly excused himself, made a phone call, and returned to let the pair know they were negotiating with the wrong team: Ringo had just been traded. Buzzie Bavasi, general manager of the Los Angeles Dodgers, had a similar reaction in 1966 when his star pitchers, Sandy Koufax and Don Drysdale, hired a Hollywood agent to represent them. The Dodgers had offered Koufax $100,00 and Drysdale $85,000 but the pair demanded that the team pay them each an annual salary of $167,000. After a brief double holdout, the team acquiesced. The Dodgers would pay Koufax $125,000 a year and Drysdale $110,000 but Bavasi refused to negotiate with their agent.

"If I gave in and began negotiating baseball contracts through an agent, then I set a precedent that's going to bring awful pain to general managers for years to come,"

Bavasi wrote in an essay he penned for *Sports Illustrated*, "because every salary negotiation with every humpty-dumpty fourth-string catcher is going to run into months of dickering." Players negotiating contracts with general managers were expected to do so alone.

A Cleveland lawyer named Mark McCormack is generally viewed as the first sports agent. His first client was Arnold Palmer, who until that point had had only his wife to help him handle the financial end of his golfing career. In 1960, when McCormack took over, Wilson Sporting Goods was earning millions each year on the Arnold Palmer golf clubs they sold, but paid Palmer only a few thousand dollars annually for the right to use his name. Heinz, the ketchup company, had paid Palmer $500 for permission to use his name and image in ads it ran in national magazines. For a cut of 10 percent, McCormack negotiated new deals that made Palmer private-jet rich. Soon McCormack was representing golfing greats Gary Player and Jack Nicklaus, and eventually skier Jean-Claude Killy. His clients were the stars, McCormack argued. They deserved a much larger share of the money.

Representation came more slowly to team sports. One pioneer was Bob Woolf, a Boston-based former criminal defense lawyer and college basketball player who declared

himself a sports agent in 1964. He claimed to have negotiated more than two thousand contracts over the next
dozen years on behalf of a long list of clients that included
Boston-area stars Carl Yastrzemski and Jim Plunkett and
also basketball great Julius Erving, who had starred at the
University of Massachusetts Amherst. Ron Shapiro was another pioneer, a Baltimore lawyer who rescued Orioles star
Brooks Robinson from a bad financial deal and then negotiated his next contract. Soon Shapiro was representing more
than half the team, including greats Jim Palmer and Eddie
Murray, and later Cal Ripken Jr.

Initially, Shapiro charged the sort of hourly rate he would
with any other client. But his law partners didn't want to
integrate baseball representation into the rest of their practice, so Shapiro created an agency. At that point he started
taking 5 percent of every contract, but then cut that to 3
percent. "We charged an additional one percent if we handled what was to me the most important thing: oversight of
finances," Shapiro said. "To teach players how to hold on to
what they earned rather than end up in bankruptcy like so
many do." Nowadays, the giant agencies such as CAA offer
financial services through a dedicated financial division, and
of course there are plenty of independent financial managers

(think Dwayne Johnson in the HBO series *Ballers*) eager to handle an athlete's money for a small annual cut.

When Steinberg was starting out, there were still signs outside some clubhouses barring agents from entry. Teams had no obligation to negotiate with agents until the early 1990s, when the collective bargaining agreement the NFL reached with the Players Association included a provision requiring them to negotiate with a player's representative if an athlete chose to hire one. A later agreement also established a certification program that required an agent to have both undergraduate and graduate degrees (typically an MBA or a law degree), submit to a background check, and pass a sixty-question multiple-choice test. Back when Steinberg got into the business, people could be agents simply by declaring themselves one.

Atlanta's management proved willing to talk to the twenty-six-year-old Steinberg about Bartkowski. But that just meant repeating what they had told his predecessor: $425,000 was a generous offer for an unproven quarterback who, the GM pointed out, had limited mobility. Steinberg took his time preparing his response. He had moved back to his parents' home in Los Angeles and set up a card table in a spare room. There, he searched for the data points that would give him the ammunition to argue that his client deserved more.

Steinberg discovered that the Falcons' offense had been pitiful the previous year, averaging less than ten points a game. That hurt ticket sales—the team drew barely ten thousand fans to its final home game—and no doubt concession revenues also plummeted for the 3-11 team. Steinberg focused on Bartkowski's potential impact on attendance and revenue. Bartkowski would juice up the listless offense, Steinberg argued, or at least lift people's hopes long enough to fill more seats for a year or two. At a time when black players were virtually barred from the quarterback position, Bartkowski was a lean, broad-shouldered white athlete who stood 6'4" tall. Steinberg, as he admitted in his 2014 autobiography, *The Agent*, shamelessly played up his friend's "blond, blue-eyed matinee-idol looks."

Steinberg asked for $750,000 a year for four years. The Falcons immediately rejected that offer, motivating Steinberg to drill down even deeper. He calculated how much more the franchise would earn even if they sold only a few thousand more tickets per game, and contemplated what it would cost the Falcons if they failed to sign Bartkowski. That, Steinberg realized, was what gave him and his client the upper hand: a fan base that would be furious if the team wasted the number-one pick. At around the time Atlanta's rookies were expected to report to training camp, the Falcons agreed to a four-year contract that paid Bartkowski $600,000 a year—a new record for an NFL rookie.

"The question is always whose reality prevails," Steinberg said. The Falcons pushed a narrative that cast Bartkowski as an unproven rookie not worth the big bucks. Steinberg countered with a narrative that cast the Falcons as a desperate franchise in need of a savior to fill the seats.

"Just saying, 'I want this dollar amount,' is no way to motivate the other side," Steinberg continued. "For starters, I'm dealing with a general manager who may have to justify a salary to an owner. So I'm helping give him the arguments to make."

STEINBERG INITIALLY FIGURED THE Bartkowski contract would be his first and last. That was before experiencing the glory of representing the NFL's top draft choice. He flew with Bartkowski to Atlanta for the contract signing. Though they landed past midnight, Steinberg said, "There were klieg lights flashing in the sky, like for a movie pre-

mier, and a huge crowd pressed up against the police line."
The pair was treated like royalty when they arrived at the
Falcons' facility to sign the contract the next day. Soon
Bartkowski was hosting his own pregame radio show and
doing ads for a local car dealership. For weeks, Steinberg
fielded calls from reporters wanting to talk to him about
the most lucrative rookie contract in NFL history. "I knew
then what I wanted to do," he said.

Steinberg earned a $30,000 commission on year one of
Bartkowski's contract but racked up $25,000 in expenses in
his first twelve months in the business. He survived his second year by maxing out his father's credit cards. He attended
an annual college all-star game, the East-West Shrine Bowl,
in search of new clients—and slept in his car to save money.
His old friend Bart swooped in to pay for a plane ticket and
pick up the cost of a rental car so Steinberg could travel
to Atlanta to recruit a promising offensive lineman at the
University of Georgia who was getting some buzz ahead of
the 1977 draft. Steinberg signed his man, allowing him to
survive another season.

He grew more systematic over the years. For starters, he
would pursue only potential stars. "As I would discover . . .
with Moon, Aikman, and Young, one superstar generates

greater interest from the press, corporations, and the public than the next fifty players combined," Steinberg wrote in *The Agent*. He started building what he calls an agent's "infrastructure"—the trainers and coaches and assistant coaches who might recommend him to a player. He was personable, quick on his feet, bold, and (maybe most important) Steve Bartkowski's agent—the agent who had negotiated a record-setting rookie deal. That's how he introduced himself to Bill Walsh when the future 49ers coach was making a name for himself at Stanford University—and one year later, he represented three players who were part of the high-octane offense Walsh had built. He still hadn't found his superstar, but he was building his client list.

Recruiting collegians had its drama. He was hungry for clients but also had limits. The recruiting process normally began with a sit-down with the family. Steinberg drew the line at the parents he met living vicariously through their athlete son to the point that they ignored their other kids. ("I felt terrible for the sisters and brothers left behind, each trying desperately to be noticed.") There were also the parents who thought their child was the best athlete on the planet, and there was no telling them otherwise. He also steered clear of those who hit him up for cash. One might say, "You know, man, I got bills," and Steinberg knew exactly what a parent was telling him: I'd be happy to consider you for my son's agent in exchange for some cash. One collegian whom Steinberg described as an "outstanding running back prospect" stopped him in front of a jewelry store and nodded to a pricey watch in the window. "If you buy me that watch," the prospect told him, "it will give you a better chance."

Over time, Steinberg carved out a kind of specialty: the community-minded player. "He stressed the value of giving back to one's community," Warren Moon later said of Steinberg, "and how he found it imperative that I, along with the rest of his clients, start charitable foundations." Early in a meeting with an athlete, Steinberg would broach the idea of devoting a small portion of the money they earned to charitable causes. It was an expression of his beliefs, and a test. He'd talk about how his father had taught him to "make a difference and change the world," and listen carefully to how a player responded. "I found I had a relatively high level of success when talking to a player who found that important," he said. He saw himself as a counselor to the whole person and not just a player's representative when negotiating with management.

"I would tell players, 'You have a platform,'" Steinberg said. "I told them, 'You could speak out against bullying, against domestic violence,' whatever it was for them." There were ethical reasons for a star athlete to give back, but Steinberg also stressed the more practical ones: the dividends it would pay in both popularity and wealth.

Steinberg found his superstar in 1978 when he landed Warren Moon as a client. Moon, the starting quarterback at the University of Washington, had gone to the same high school as Steinberg, who stressed the connection in a hand-written note introducing himself to Moon. Steinberg rarely attended college games; his standard line to prospects was always, "Would you rather that next fall I be at your football game in the NFL and have dinner with you the night before, or that I attend a college game to recruit players for the following draft?" But he bought a ticket to see Moon play during his senior year, when Washington came to the Bay Area to play Cal. He knew right then that he had to have him as a client.

Recruiting Moon was no easy task. He played his final game in the Rose Bowl, where he earned game MVP. Steinberg estimated that he spoke to Moon fifty times over a three-month period before the quarterback finally committed to him. He took solace in the fact that Moon was still returning his calls. "I was overwhelmed by his dignity, maturity, wisdom, and attention to detail," Steinberg wrote in *The Agent*. Moon's skill at networking also impressed him. That would serve him well both as a player and in life after football.

Success in landing Moon meant sharing the frustrations that were the first half dozen years of his career. Moon was a quarterback, but he was also black. Would he consider changing positions, teams asked Steinberg, and play running back or receiver or defensive back? "If he were open to that idea, they assured me, he would go much higher in the draft," Steinberg said. Instead, Moon signed with the Edmonton Eskimos in the Canadian Football League. The $35,000 signing bonus and $35,000 salary he negotiated on Moon's behalf, Steinberg said, was "a better deal financially than what we projected he would have received in the NFL." There would be no denying his quarterbacking skills after he led the Eskimos to Grey Cup championships (the CFL's Super Bowl) in five of his six years in the league. Belatedly, the NFL noticed that Moon, then twenty-seven, was as marketable (handsome, poised, a winning smile to match a winning personality) as he was talented at the quarterback position. "I knew I had a bidding war situation," Steinberg said.

The upstart AFL had taken on the established NFL in the 1960s and helped Joe Namath earn an unprecedented $427,000 a year—more than double what he would have been paid if he'd signed with the NFL's Cardinals, which had selected him twelfth in the 1965 draft. The players lost that leverage one year later when the two leagues merged and all eight original AFL teams were absorbed by the NFL. As luck would have it, the United States Football League, or USFL, was founded the year before Moon's Canadian contract ended. (During the four years of the USFL's existence, the average player's salary in the NFL more than doubled, from $90,000 to $190,000.)

Steinberg confessed that he had no idea what Moon might be worth on the open market. So the two took to the road in 1983 for the "Moon sweepstakes." In Houston, the Oilers' owner drove them to an oil well and said, "This could be yours." The owner of the Tampa Bay Buccaneers took them up in a steel high-rise under construction and asked Moon how he'd like to have the money "to have a floor or two of this building." In New York they met with, among others, Donald Trump, who owned the USFL's New Jersey

Generals. Steinberg was hoping that Trump, just as the owner of the New York Jets had done two decades earlier with Namath, could set the outer bounds for a quarterback's salary. Steinberg and his client were shown the "Trump Experience," Steinberg remembered, and then had a "cordial" sit-down with the future president. But it was obvious that he would not be investing millions in Warren Moon when "he had already committed a fortune to the team." The pair also traveled to Honolulu for the Pro Bowl, where they met with the coach of the Seattle Seahawks. Seattle was Moon's sentimental choice. He had gone to college there and still lived in the area during the off-season.

Moon chose the Oilers (now the Tennessee Titans) over the Seahawks. Both teams offered him the same five-year, $5.5 million contract, but Seattle's front office refused to guarantee the money. If he had signed with Seattle, he would have gotten paid if he were hurt, Moon explained in an interview with the *New York Times*. "But, say, if I came in and was a total bust or something like that, they could have gotten rid of me because there was a big salary involved." Either way, Steinberg crowed to the *Times*, Moon's was "the biggest football contract of all time."

That was terrific news for his client, of course, but also

for Steinberg, who found himself fielding calls from reporters wanting to write about the young agent who had hammered out the record deal. "The Agent in the White Hat," read the headline over a feature in the *Los Angeles Times*. Profiles followed in the *San Francisco Chronicle*, *Playboy*, and *People* magazine.

AGENTS AT THAT TIME were usually lawyers who dressed accordingly, in suit and tie, as if going to court. Steinberg, by contrast, wore jeans, surfer shirts, and boat shoes. "He was a very laid-back guy, as California as you could be," Moon told one profiler. Invariably, Steinberg was younger than the parents who often served as the first line of defense for the players he was recruiting, but, he said, despite a baby face that made him look even younger than he was, that never seemed to be an issue. "My age made it that much easier for me to connect to the actual client I'd be counseling," he said, adding, "any person looking for a traditional agent with nine pinky rings and slicked-back hair wasn't the kind of client I was looking for anyway."

Yet the person Steinberg seemed to most zealously represent was himself. To help raise his profile, he hired a publicist. *Cosmopolitan* named him a "Bachelor of the Year," and he was a contestant on *The Dating Game*. He fell in love with a home in the Berkeley hills that he admitted he couldn't afford, but this was before the NFL Players Association had a rule forbidding an agent from borrowing money from a player; Warren Moon and a second client loaned him the down payment on a four-level house with floor-to-ceiling windows and panoramic views of the Bay Area.

Steinberg broadened his practice to include news anchors and sports broadcasters. A former Falcons teammate of Bartkowski's sought to get into coaching, and so Steinberg began representing football coaches. The practice was growing too large for one person to handle, and so, in 1981, six years after taking on Steve Bartkowski as his first client, Steinberg hired another agent, Mike Sullivan, a "bright young lawyer" he had found at the accounting firm Arthur Andersen LLP. That same year he hired his first secretary.

Steinberg's encounters with management were still hit-and-miss. He flew to Green Bay to negotiate a contract on behalf of an offensive lineman the Packers had chosen with the seventh overall pick in the 1985 draft. "Oh, another agent's in town," the Packers coach told reporters in advance of Steinberg's arrival. He suggested that he might invite

Steinberg over for dinner, adding, "My wife will cook rat poison."

Other agents were proving no more collegial. Steinberg thought he had the inside track on another potential number-one draft pick until the prospect abruptly cut off communications. When the two finally spoke weeks later, the recruit said his father had been scared off by a rival agent who had supposedly told him that he would be committing malpractice as a father if he let his son sign with Steinberg. "These other agents called me a publicity hound, which was outrageous," he wrote in *The Agent*. Should he hang up on reporters when they called him, he asked plaintively, or leave their voice mails unreturned? Instead of being resentful, he said, "they should've thanked me for lifting the image of a profession that, let's face it, wasn't exactly known for its integrity." He told me of the time he and a second agent, who was black, were recruiting the same star tight end. The other agent introduced himself to Steinberg as the tight end's uncle, and the young hotshot from California gave him his entire spiel in a hotel lobby the day before that year's Senior Bowl. The incident seemed comical, but Steinberg was furious over the deception.

Steve Young became a client around the time Warren

Moon was entering the NFL. Young had just finished his final season quarterbacking for Brigham Young University, where he averaged three touchdown passes per game, and his 71 percent completion rate set an NCAA single-season record. Not surprisingly, Steinberg fell hard when the two met at the Salt Lake City airport in 1984. A direct descendant of Brigham Young himself and a devout Mormon, this was one potential recruit who didn't hesitate when Steinberg suggested that he see himself as a role model. "Without a doubt," Young said earnestly.

There would be no need for a national tour like Steinberg had done with Moon. The GM of the LA Express of the USFL "had his eyes on Steve before I did." The deal Steinberg negotiated on his client's behalf included a $5 million signing bonus and a $37 million salary to be paid over several decades. That $42 million deal was "undoubtedly the richest contract in the history of sports," Steinberg wrote in his book, but Young, with a rueful laugh, told an interviewer years later that he didn't see much of that money, only the grief of having been pegged by the media as the "$40 million man." The contract had been a bet on the USFL; if that league had succeeded in the fashion of the AFL a couple of decades earlier, then Young would have had a deal worth

$42 million. But the LA Express suspended operations only one year after signing Young, and the USFL folded not long after that. In time, Young again became the "$40 million man," this time for real, when Steinberg negotiated a six-year, $45 million deal on his behalf with the San Francisco 49ers that made him the highest-paid player in football.

Steinberg moved into baseball in 1985 when he partnered with Jeff Moorad, another young agent in the Bay Area. In time, the newly formed Steinberg & Moorad would represent Will Clark, Manny Ramirez, CC Sabathia, Mo Vaughn, and Ivan "Pudge" Rodriguez, among other big-name baseball stars. When Steinberg got married that year, Steve Young and Warren Moon stood as two of his groomsmen, while Steve Bartkowski was his best man. There was a momentary speed bump when, on day two of his Maui honeymoon, he learned that Mike Sullivan had left the practice after soliciting clients at the wedding. From Hawaii, Steinberg frantically phoned every player he thought Sullivan might try to poach. In the end he lost several clients, but no stars.

With success, Steinberg grew bolder in asserting himself in the lives of his players. He taught them about networking and encouraged them to start thinking about life after the game. It seemed like he would be the most irritating companion at an awards banquet. "I want you to be able to tell me who everyone in the room is," he would tell clients. "I want you to shake their hands and ask for their cards, and when you get back to your room, I want you to write on the back of each card some way to remember that individual." He discouraged them from driving when they'd been drinking and instructed them on the proper way to apologize if they were caught. "You look people right in the eye and say you're sorry," he explained. "You say you've learned your lesson and this won't happen again."

Steinberg represented the number-one picks in the 1989 and 1990 NFL drafts (quarterbacks Troy Aikman and Jeff George) and then again in 1991 (defensive standout Russell Maryland). By that time, he had moved to Southern California and opened an office in Newport Beach, not far from the ocean. He and Moorad hired another agent who was adept at analytics. This new hire tracked the economics of every team and logged performance statistics for every player in the league. "You try to construct a rationale based on the numbers for why a player ought to be paid what you're asking for," Steinberg said. "You find similarly situated players in terms of age, position, and productivity. You look at factors like performance on the field and the team's performance. The aim is to show how your player is much more productive than [an initial] salary offer would suggest."

Normally, Steinberg negotiated with the general manager or someone else in the front office. But Jerry Jones, then the new owner of the Cowboys, chose to meet directly with Steinberg when Dallas chose Troy Aikman with the first overall pick. Their first meeting lasted into the early morning hours and left Steinberg feeling like he'd discovered a kindred spirit. That began the first of what Steinberg called "deep friendships" with several of football's more high-profile (and controversial) owners: Jones; Robert "Bob" Kraft, who bought the Patriots in 1994; and Dan Snyder, who purchased the Washington Redskins in 1999. Each possessed what Steinberg dubbed "the same pioneering spirit." Each, to Steinberg's mind, recognized that the players, and by extension their agents, were less adversaries and more allies on behalf of football in its competition with the other forms of entertainment, including Disney and HBO. Grow the television pie and everyone benefits. Steinberg's tack with Jones was to get him to imagine what his franchise could do with Aikman, a "quarterback with movie-star looks and a name out of central casting." The two agreed on a six-year,

$11.2 million deal—at that time, the largest contract ever for an NFL rookie.

The year 1993 proved a pivotal one for football, and especially for an agent with a growing practice. The league had recently hammered out deals with the various television networks that paid a combined $900 million a year for the rights to broadcast NFL games. At the same time, the league was under legal pressure to reform a system that gave athletes little say over where they lived and worked. The NFL's answer was the institution of unrestricted free agency in exchange for a salary cap for players with less than five years of experience (that figure was later lowered to four years). After that time, a player could sell his services to the highest bidder. With teams competing each year for talented veterans, salaries began an inexorable climb. That first year Steinberg negotiated two record-setting contracts on behalf of veteran clients. The first, for former league MVP Thurman Thomas of the Buffalo Bills, was a four-year, $13.5 million deal that made him the league's highest-paid running back. The second, negotiated on behalf of All-Pro safety Tim McDonald for $2.5 million per year, made him the highest-paid defensive back in league history. Steinberg had the number-one pick again in 1993, and in 1994 and 1995.

Cameron Crowe was just starting his research for a movie he was writing about sports agents around the time of the 1993 draft. Steinberg invited Crowe to the draft, where his client Drew Bledsoe, a quarterback, was the number-one pick, and let Crowe join them when they flew to Boston to introduce Bledsoe to the local press. Then Steinberg hosted Crowe during Super Bowl week and again at a pro scouting day. Maybe most significant, Steinberg brought him to an owners' meeting in Palm Desert, California, where he met Tim McDonald, the player who inspired the line "Show me the money." As McDonald remembered it, Crowe was in the room when, frustrated with the low offers he had been hearing all day as a free agent, he said, less memorably, "Somebody's going to have to show me some money." The filmmaker even used pictures he borrowed from Steinberg showing him standing next to different players (later superimposing Tom Cruise's face over Steinberg's) to create the film-set version of an agent's office.

Steinberg walked the red carpet at the West-Coast premiere of the movie in 1996. He walked it again in New York for its East-Coast opening. Director Oliver Stone then asked for his help while working on the movie *Any Given Sunday*, and Steinberg also worked as a consultant on *Arli$$*, an HBO show about a sports agent with flexible morals.

Steinberg's practice was thriving as the 1990s came to an end, bringing in millions in fees each year. His firm represented eighty-six NFL players in 1999, along with numerous baseball players and the stray basketball client Steinberg had picked up since agreeing to represent Greg Anthony, a gifted point guard who'd played at the University of Nevada, Las Vegas. Steinberg also represented two of boxing's biggest names, Lennox Lewis and Oscar De La Hoya, and also Olympian Brian Boitano.

It wasn't about the money, Steinberg liked to say. It was never about the money. But that was before David Falk, who represented Michael Jordan, among other basketball stars, sold his practice in 1998 for $100 million. A year later, Assante, a financial management company based in Canada, offered $120 million to buy Steinberg & Moorad, which had recently taken on a third partner and renamed itself Steinberg, Moorad & Dunn. Moorad was in favor of selling, and besides, the Assante deal meant Steinberg would clear somewhere between $30 million and $40 million after taxes. He said yes.

2

The Visionary

Don Yee knows it makes no sense that he ended up as a football agent. Baseball had always been his sport growing up in Sacramento, California. At thirteen, he was the batboy for the local Triple-A baseball team, where he also washed the players' uniforms and kept the clubhouse refrigerator stocked with drinks. He went to college at UCLA, where basketball became his obsession. He arrived in Los Angeles the same year as Magic Johnson. Yee had interned at a sports radio show in Sacramento and used that connection to secure press credentials to cover the Lakers' home games during Magic's rookie season. He was only eighteen years old, yet was sitting only a few seats from legendary Lakers announcer Chick Hearn.

"From an agent's standpoint, football is the least lucrative, and it's the highest risk," Yee said. Its average salaries are lower than those of other sports, and its players have higher injury rates. The short life span of the typical NFL career (under four years) means constantly finding new recruits to replace those who are no longer in the game. NFL salaries aren't guaranteed the way they are in baseball and basketball, and the NFL players union is probably the least effective in all the major sports. "From a business standpoint, an agent can make much more doing baseball or basketball or soccer," Yee said.

Yet familiarity turned him off to baseball. "Baseball as a business means you're basically arguing statistics," he said. That might be interesting to some, but not to him. "Baseball players don't generally have a team-oriented psychology," Yee said. "Your typical baseball player is thinking, 'I only have to focus on my own statistics, because that's how I get paid. If I play third base, I don't have to care about how the right fielder does.'" Soccer he rejected because he didn't know the sport, and basketball seemed too great a stretch for a first-generation Asian kid raised in Sacramento. "Basketball is a completely different culture," he said.

That left football, which felt right despite the economic arguments against it. Football players can be as obsessed with their personal stats as any athlete, but they know that, fundamentally, they need to work together as a unit to attain any kind of success. "The players understand that," Yee said. "And I felt it may be easier to work with people with that kind of mind-set." So, in 1987, at twenty-seven years old, he gained his certification and went looking for the players who might help him build a practice.

"I didn't play football," Yee said. "I wasn't the son of a coach. I wasn't in the same dorm as a player. No one knew me."

YEE WAS IN THE fifth grade when the idea of becoming an agent first planted itself in his head. He loved baseball, and he loved watching reruns of an old television legal drama called *Perry Mason*. And so when his teacher asked the class to write an essay about what they wanted to be when they grew up, Yee merged the two. "Basically, I imagined myself as Willie Mays's lawyer," he said over breakfast at a café just east of Los Angeles, where he lives and works. A fit, friendly man in his fifties, Yee was dressed casually in a blue polo shirt, gray jeans, and black shoes. Not once in our two hours together did he so much as glance at his phone. Maybe Tom Brady was trying to reach him, or Julian Edelman, or Jimmy Garoppolo, or Sean Payton. I mentioned the missing phone, and Yee, looking me in the eye, noted that I had come a long way to speak with him. As a "courtesy," he said, he had packed it away in the black satchel he carried with him.

There was a time when Yee wanted nothing to do with sports. "You see what it's really like at a young age, and—well, I felt I had seen enough," he said. He earned a law degree at the University of Virginia School of Law and found a job handling civil suits on behalf of businesses. "After a year of that, I decided to get [football] certification," he said.

The first client is the hardest. Without one, there's no answer to the inevitable question of who an agent represents. Yee found his, a Boise State University wide receiver named Tony Hunter, watching television. He saw that Hunter had star potential and liked that he played for a lower-profile school. Their games were rarely on TV, and then probably only in a few western states, which meant less competition. Doing his research, Yee learned that Hunter was from Reno, Nevada, just over two hours' drive from Sacramento.

"Tony gave me the chance to work with him," Yee said. Hunter was barely bigger than Yee—he stood 5'8" tall and weighed only 160 pounds—and never made it in the NFL. But Yee secured him a contract to play in the Canadian Football League, where he spent four years as a kick and punt returner and part-time wide receiver. "It was then that I realized there's a lot of gravity to this role I was taking on," Yee said. "I [had] just talked a guy into going to another country to play . . . a very different game. Sending his life on a different course. You realize you're not dealing with widgets," he said. "You're dealing with human beings."

Being Asian, Yee understood, would hurt him as a recruiter. Social psychology studies show that people generally feel more comfortable with those who are like themselves. That's just human nature. "A white quarterback with a white agent—they might have been in similar fraternities, had more similar life experiences. It's an easier bridge to cross to create a comfortable familiarity," Yee said. "A lot of guys that play college football are in a fraternity, black or white. They may not have much exposure to Asians." He had earned a law degree at a top law school, if that mattered. But he was also low-key and not the type to camp out in a hotel lobby. "That's not my personality," he said. "I don't want to conduct my business like that." His single advantage, he realized, was what he's come to call his "superpower": an ability to watch a game for only a short period and identify a potential NFLer.

For as long as he can remember, Yee said, he'd had a room outfitted with multiple televisions. These days he has eight in his den. He follows the same Saturday ritual during college football season, one he established when he was just starting out. He's in the den by 10:00 a.m. to catch the first games from the East Coast, and stays there through the completion of the West-Coast games. A favorite moment for him was the day half a dozen years ago when, still groggy, he turned on his TVs, plopped onto the couch, and immediately zeroed in on a tight end for the University of Tennessee. He didn't know anything about him other than his uniform number, but, he said, in less than five minutes of watching, he knew: "He's an NFL guy." That's how he first noticed Mychal Rivera, an eventual sixth-round pick whose four-year career as a receiver for the Oakland Raiders was cut short by injury.

The rest of Yee's formula is due diligence. "Once I know I'm looking at someone with NFL potential, it's time to do some homework," he said. "Is he a nice person? Is he reasonably intelligent?" In other words, is this someone he could work with?

Yee's TV room was where he first spotted Tom Brady. Six Super Bowl rings later, Brady is recognized even by casual football fans as one of the best quarterbacks of all time. Yet he spent his first two years at the University of Michigan on the bench, and became the full-time starter only midway through his senior year. His breakout game was the 2000 Orange Bowl, when he led Michigan to a dramatic win over the University of Alabama on national television. Still, Brady was the 199th pick when the Patriots chose him in the sixth round of the 2000 draft.

Julian Edelman provides an even better example of Yee's superpower. Edelman had no New Year's Day heroics to vault him into prominence. He played in relative obscurity as the starting quarterback for Kent State University. "He was not on the radar coming out of college," Yee said. "But we saw something." When Edelman ran with the ball, he averaged just under five yards per carry, and had scored twenty-two touchdowns. He even occasionally punted the ball, amassing a decent average of thirty-eight yards per kick. Edelman was a football player, even if he wasn't destined to be a starting quarterback in the NFL. "My job at that point was getting people to see the vision for him," Yee said. He made a list of franchises he thought might be interested in Edelman and worked the phone in search of a team that would at least listen.

The Patriots chose Edelman with their seventh and final pick of the 2009 draft. He probably wouldn't have even made the team if not for a seventy-five-yard punt return during a meaningless preseason game. He had several good games at receiver as a rookie, but he was primarily a special-teams player during his first several years in the league, ranking second in punt returns his second year. Early in his career, he even filled in as defensive back on a Patriots club depleted by injuries. By 2013, his fifth year in the league, he was a top-five receiver with 105 receptions and more than a thousand yards. He was MVP of the 2019 Super Bowl after a game-high ten catches for 141 yards.

"The thing that was so rewarding [about seeing] Julian win the Super Bowl MVP award was knowing that we had a specific vision as well as a specific path and dots that we wanted to try to connect," Yee said. It's Edelman, of course, who deserves credit for having the talent and the work ethic to succeed, Yee stressed. But he was also proud of the part he has played in Edelman's success.

Yee has spotted any number of players by watching his TVs. Many have gone on to play for a decade or more in the NFL, if not quite as famously as his two best-known clients. Position makes no difference, Yee said. He's as likely to notice an NFL-caliber lineman as he is an athlete playing one of the so-called talent positions (quarterback, running back, receiver). Television is how he first spotted Larry Allen, for instance, an offensive lineman from Sonoma State University in California who was enshrined in the Hall of Fame in 2013 after a fourteen-year career in the NFL.

"Each year the scouts come up with their list of the top fifty or top one hundred. Well, not according to me," Yee said. He occasionally competes for a consensus top pick, but mainly he has fashioned a career out of representing those who make no one's list of top prospects. "I have tremendous confidence in my ability to identify talent," he said, adding, "I wish I was better at something else, frankly. Unfortunately, I'm not good at ninety-nine-point-nine percent of the things that exist out there."

Other than as a sports agent, how else could he make a living and have any fun doing it, except maybe as a low-paid scout or a front-office suit?

3

The Shark

Drew Rosenhaus knew he wanted to be a sports agent practically from birth. "I was born to be an agent," he repeats several times in *A Shark Never Sleeps: Wheeling and Dealing with the NFL's Most Ruthless Agent*, the memoir he wrote less than a decade after he entered the business. "I was born to dominate in this business from the day my parents brought me home from the hospital."

Growing up in Miami, Rosenhaus studied stat sheets as though he were a pro scout and, when he was thirteen years old, ditched school the first time ESPN broadcast the draft on television, in 1980. He was still a teenager when he had his family's housekeeper take him and his brother to watch a Dolphins practice. Stopped by a security guard, Rosenhaus said they were the nephews of Reggie Roby. The guard waved them through, though Roby is black and Rosenhaus is white. "They got in," Michael Bamberger wrote in a profile of Rosenhaus that ran in *Sports Illustrated* in 1996, "and Drew has been coloring the truth ever since."

Rosenhaus attended the University of Miami, where the football team had been crowned national champions the year before he arrived. There, he studied hard and searched for ways to ingratiate himself with the team's best players. His big break came during his freshman year, when he found himself in the same class as a player whose cousin was the team's star fullback, future NFLer Alonzo Highsmith. Rosenhaus offered Highsmith's cousin whatever help he might need with the course. In turn, his new friend promised to introduce him to others on the team. "I would tutor them," Rosenhaus said. "I would prepare them for exams. I would help them write papers."

Rosenhaus was a self-described rich kid who drove a Porsche and lived in a big house along the water. He'd invite the players to hang out there, where the refrigerator was always stocked. He brought them to his parents' country club and took them out on his cousin's boat. Rain or shine, he told them, he was ready to give any of them a ride to class or anywhere they needed to go. Among those he got to know that way was the team's star wide receiver, Michael Irvin. "Drew, if you were older and had a little bit of experience, I'd hire you to be my agent," Rosenhaus said Irvin told him when the future Hall of Famer was at his house for a tutoring session.

Law school seemed the wisest route for a wannabe agent. That's what Steinberg had done nearly twenty years earlier, and then Yee a decade after that. Rosenhaus went to the Duke University School of Law, a school he had chosen because a professor there had written a textbook about sports law, and because he imagined graduating from a top-ranked school would give him an advantage over the competition. Rosenhaus was still a first-year law student when he decided his goal was a job with Mel Levine, a Fort Lauderdale–based agent who signed several of the top Miami players Rosenhaus had befriended on campus, including Michael Irvin. Rosenhaus phoned Levine three times a day for a month, and then, when that failed, flew to Miami to track down

Irvin and get him to put in a good word with his agent. Rosenhaus figured he must have phoned Levine another few hundred times before the agent finally invited him to his office in the spring of 1989.

On the day of the meeting, Rosenhaus put on his best suit, slicked back his hair, and even splurged on a barbershop shave—and then wondered why he had bothered. He described Levine as a short, shlubby guy dressed in jeans and a short-sleeved shirt. "I knew at that instant that I would dominate the business," Rosenhaus recalled. "This little dork and his fellow agents couldn't compete with a shark like myself." Levine told him he would pay him $250 a week and cover his expenses, along with a 25 percent cut of any fees his recruits generated. Looking Levine in the eye, Rosenhaus told him it was a day he would never forget—and began plotting his exit strategy before he even reached his car, he confessed in his memoir. "He had let the shark into the fishpond," Rosenhaus wrote. (Levine later served more than two years in prison on tax and bank fraud charges unrelated to his job as a sports agent.)

Rosenhaus made himself indispensable in his brief time with Levine. He acknowledged that he learned a lot from Levine, a lawyer and CPA, but often felt more like the

teacher than the student. That summer, Rosenhaus told Levine about a highly touted wide receiver at Syracuse University who hadn't yet signed with an agent, but Levine complained that he had no idea how to reach the player. Showing his boss how it was done, Rosenhaus phoned the Syracuse athletic department and, pretending to be the player's tutor, said he needed his number to arrange a time to help him prep for a test. To reach other potential clients, Rosenhaus pretended to be a classmate, an NFL scout, a family member—anything to get a phone number. He returned to Durham for his second year of law school intent on signing as many players as he could once the season had ended.

Rosenhaus inked deals with five collegians on Levine's behalf. The best of them was Robert Massey, a hard-hitting cornerback who played for North Carolina Central University, a small, historically black school five minutes from Duke. Rosenhaus arranged an appearance for the two on ESPN and then acted as if he were Massey's agent, without so much as mentioning Levine or his firm's name. "This was my chance to hype myself as my own man, and I went for it," Rosenhaus explained.

Levine, of course, was furious. "He thought I stabbed him in the heart," Rosenhaus wrote in *A Shark Never Sleeps*. "But

business was business. I had outgrown him in a short period." Rosenhaus poached Massey and cast himself as noble for allowing Levine to keep the other four prospects he had recruited to his agency. Then Rosenhaus expressed outrage when Marvin Demoff, then one of football's top agents, tried to steal Massey from him. Rosenhaus had met Demoff at a college all-star game and gushed about wanting to be like the senior agent. A few days later, the more experienced agent phoned Massey to ask him why he wasn't going with the real deal instead of some young wannabe. "Stabbed in the back," Rosenhaus wrote unironically in his book. Massey, however, stuck with Rosenhaus, who represented the talented cornerback when the Saints chose him in the second round of the 1989 draft.

Today we call it "white privilege": Rosenhaus was a twenty-two-year-old law student, yet a bank gave him a $40,000 line of credit to fund a new agency he was calling Rosenhaus Sports Representation. He set up shop in his mother's interior design office and, because he still needed to finish his final year at Duke, deputized his younger brother, who was more or less following his older brother's playbook. He, too, was at the University of Miami, where he ingratiated himself with the football team's star players by dangling access to the Miami Beach lifestyle their family money granted them.

At that point, Rosenhaus had only a single client—but that proved to be enough when *USA Today* declared Massey the most interesting pick of the draft. Rosenhaus used the line to convince reporters at both the *Miami Herald* and the *South Florida Sun-Sentinel* to write about the law school student who had signed him. He and Massey were guests on a TV show hosted by a prominent south Florida sportscaster, which led to more media appearances. "But I wanted more," Rosenhaus recounted in his book. "Like a shark smelling blood, I went into a media frenzy." His negotiations with the Saints would be his first as an agent, but Rosenhaus invited ESPN to film the haggling—and then started spreading the word among the reporters he had recently befriended. The Saints had to invite the television cameras into their offices or look scared of this brash newbie.

Rosenhaus's adversary was Saints GM Jim Finks, a hard-nosed negotiator and one of football's more well-regarded executives. Salaries in the NFL are "slotted," which in agentspeak means a player's pay is set by his position in the draft. The Saints intended to pay Massey what any NFL team would pay a second-rounder who had been the forty-second pick in the draft. But Rosenhaus argued that the buzz around Massey (buzz that he had played a central role in creating, of course) demonstrated that his client should be paid like a first-rounder, a point he hammered on over and over again in his negotiations with Finks. The resulting footage, *Sports Illustrated*'s Bamberger wrote, was "painful": Rosenhaus talking nonstop while the camera occasionally pans to a silent, cross-armed Finks, who looked either angry or anguished. "I thought if I didn't let him talk, I couldn't look bad," Rosenhaus later explained.

Finks wasn't budging, however, and Rosenhaus's first client became a holdout before he had played a single down of pro football. Massey eventually signed, but the deal seemed more about Rosenhaus saving face than about helping his client. If the Saints insisted on paying Massey as a second-rounder, Rosenhaus insisted that his client sign a two-year contract for $600,000 a year rather than the customary three- or four-year deal, though that meant a smaller signing bonus. Massey started every game he played in his first two years with the Saints—who then traded him to the 4–12 Phoenix (later Arizona) Cardinals.

"When the time for a second contract arrived, we weren't going to deal with it," Bill Kuharich, then the Saints' director of player personnel, told *Sports Illustrated*. "We decided to move Robert [Massey] not solely because of Drew, but he was certainly a big factor."

There were more missteps in Rosenhaus's first full year as an agent, which he described in his book in a chapter called "Second Place Sucks." From reading the same prognostications that everyone else did he learned about Ray Agnew, a top-rated defensive lineman at North Carolina State University. Rosenhaus visited Agnew's family in North Carolina and then, once Agnew had played his last college game, flew him to Miami to show him a good time. He put him up in one of the city's pricier hotels and thought he had scored when, after a night of partying that ended in a strip club, Agnew told Rosenhaus he was ready to sign. But by the time Rosenhaus got to the hotel the next day, Agnew had already checked out. Later he learned that Agnew, the number-ten pick in the 1990 draft, had been talking simultaneously with other agents. "I learned a key lesson," Rosenhaus wrote in *A Shark Never Sleeps.* "You must sign the player on the spot if he is ready. Don't give him a chance to change his mind."

There would be more hard-earned lessons, like when he signed Randal Hill, a star wide receiver at the University of Miami whom the Dolphins took with their first-round pick. A lifelong Dolphins fan, Rosenhaus was thrilled that the Fins had chosen Hill, a local kid born and raised in Miami. But the Dolphins insisted on a four-year contract, and Rosenhaus had Hill hold out for a three-year deal. He thought he and his client had won when, after a twenty-seven-day holdout, the Dolphins gave Hill his three-year deal. Then, one game into the season, the team traded him to Phoenix. "That flight to Arizona was the worst of my life," Rosenhaus confessed. Back home, the sports pages and sports radio jockeys were blaming Rosenhaus for the banishment of the hometown hero. "I was crushed and humiliated," he said, but added, "As an agent, it is critical always, without exception, to be positive. You will be tested time and time again, and you must always keep your head high."

Rosenhaus was nothing if not persistent. He may not have Don Yee's superpower, but there's no denying his drive and will. "With every ounce and fiber of my being, I sold and sold myself," he said. He studied the market and read everything he could get his hands on, including the tout sheets and insider-y newsletters that produced mock drafts and ranked draftees by position. Every scout Rosenhaus came across became a friend, along with any coach, assistant coach, or factotum, so long as he or she was connected to a college athletic program or an NFL club. His quarry was the top picks, even though he knew that there might be dozens, if not hundreds, of agents pursuing those prospects—but that's exactly where Rosenhaus felt he belonged. "Handsome, well-dressed, smooth talker, polished, professional, well-educated, confident, and cool as a cucumber," he boasted in his book.

Early in his career, Rosenhaus seemed to have cornered the market on stars from his alma mater. He had grown accustomed to going anywhere he wanted on the Miami campus. That changed after a new coaching staff took over and discovered Rosenhaus hanging around the gym where players worked out. Soon the school had a new rule: agents had to notify the administration whenever they were on campus. But Rosenhaus still had his younger brother Jason, who continued on to law school there. As a student, he was free to go wherever he wanted. "He did exactly as we planned he would," Rosenhaus wrote. With his brother still on campus, Rosenhaus continued to land Miami players as clients.

Over time, Rosenhaus discovered the downside of representing recruits straight out of college. "These are college kids," Rosenhaus wrote. "Many are unpredictable." It was different with those who had already established themselves in the NFL. Among the veterans he picked up early on was Jeff Cross, a star defensive lineman for the Dolphins through the first half of the 1990s. Another player Rosenhaus knew told him that Cross had just fired his agent. Rosenhaus and his brother jumped into the car to go find Cross at a Fort Lauderdale nightclub. Rosenhaus invited him over to chat. The bar tab ran to hundreds of dollars, but it was worth it. He had added a local star to his client list.

"I didn't only want the money," Rosenhaus wrote. "I wanted the lifestyle."

The typical player remains loyal to a single agent, and the better agents seem to lose a client only occasionally. Established players were paid more than rookies, yet there was less competition for veterans than there was for the hottest college prospects. This exploitable fact became Rosenhaus's specialty: poaching veterans to build a practice. "I was making my move to the top," Rosenhaus wrote of the mid-1990s.

There are good reasons to change agents: there are bad agents out there, or at least agents who aren't quite as good as the best, so there are always unhappy veterans looking for new representation. "My rule is never to approach anyone who already has an agent," said Tory Dandy. "I don't believe in soliciting guys already under representation." Rosenhaus, however, adopted a different policy. At one point, he represented nineteen Dolphins, almost all of them veterans he wooed by picking up the tab at one south Florida hot spot or another. His MO was always the same: if he knew a player was making, say, $1.2 million a year, he might whisper in their ear that they were really worth $1.5 million, if not $1.8 million. Then he'd go for the pitch: No two people will work harder than my brother and me, he'd say, speed-talking his way through his spiel. He would be there for them twenty-four seven. And there would never be anybody in the middle of their relationship. Even as his practice grew, Rosenhaus never hired anyone to answer his phone.

"I'm not married, I have no kids, I don't take vacations," he would tell a recruit. "I literally work seven days a week." In short order, Rosenhaus had convinced a series of All-Pro players (Eric Green of the Pittsburgh Steelers, Mo Lewis of the Jets, Brian Blades of the Seahawks, and his brother Bennie of the Detroit Lions) to let him negotiate for them now that they were ready to become free agents. "If you hear me talk to a team about my player, you would think I'm representing a god," Rosenhaus said. One of his more impressive deals during this period was on behalf of Leon Searcy, another veteran Rosenhaus came to represent. In 1996, Searcy signed a $17 million contract, including a $5 million signing bonus, making him the highest-paid offensive lineman in the NFL.

There are consequences when an agent's specialty is taking clients from rivals rather than pursuing unsigned collegians, however. At some point in the 1990s, the league began requiring anyone who wished to remain certified to attend an annual NFL Players Association agent meeting. At one of the first of these meetings, Tim Irwin stood up to denounce Rosenhaus and his brother. Irwin had only recently become an agent after a fourteen-year career as an NFL offensive lineman. He described the Rosenhauses as a "cancer" on the business and demanded that the players union sanction them. "He said we lure guys away by taking them out to nightclubs and impressing them with women," remembered Rosenhaus. He dismissed the criticism as bad blood because Irwin had lost a client to them a year earlier and, Rosenhaus being Rosenhaus, turned the rebuke into a boast. He told of the standing ovation the other agents gave Irwin when he was done talking with pride, and wrote, "Never before had an agent been singled out in a seminar and teamed up on by all the other agents there."

In 1996, *Sports Illustrated* put Rosenhaus's picture on its cover and declared him "The Most Hated Man in Pro Football." The magazine had no trouble finding agents willing to criticize Rosenhaus on the record. "The biggest scumbag in the business," said an agent named Peter Schaffer, who had lost a client on the Dolphins to Rosenhaus. "When you look up sleazeball agent in the dictionary, there's a picture of Drew with his slicked-back hair," said Craig Fenech, who represented the Dolphins' popular placekicker Pete Stoyanovich until losing him to Rosenhaus. Several agents confessed in interviews with the magazine that they grew nervous if a client signed with the Dolphins, knowing he would then be living in Rosenhaus's backyard. "He doesn't know how to take no for an answer," said a third agent who lost a Dolphin client to Rosenhaus.

How some of Rosenhaus's clients fared is more disturbing than anything a rival agent might say about him. *Sports Illustrated* offered what its writer called the "troubling case" of Dolphins safety Louis Oliver. Oliver's original agent had negotiated a three-year deal with the Dolphins at $1.4 million a year, but Rosenhaus, the magazine reported, was telling him he deserved $2 million. Oliver, who loved Miami, fired his agent and went with Rosenhaus, who got him not $2 million but $1.6 million per year with the Cincinnati Bengals. After playing poorly in Cincinnati, Oliver ended up back in Miami, playing for the league minimum of $178,000 per year.

Rosenhaus denied that he mismanaged Oliver's career. He readily confessed, though, that he fibbed to Dolphins management when, in 1995, he negotiated a free-agent deal with the club on behalf of tight end Eric Green. If Miami believed him when he implied that another team had topped their $1.88 million per year offer, then that was the fault of the executives who failed to check with the NFL, which kept a clearinghouse of such information. Rosenhaus did his job, getting Miami to up its offer to $2 million a year.

"I'm not going to lie constantly," he told the magazine. "I'm not a pathological liar. But in some instances, I'll bluff." Besides, he added, "Teams are not supposed to believe agents." It was probably an honest expression of his view of the profession but was diametrically opposed to what might be seen as the agent code: your word is all you have in a profession that's all about reputation and trust.

But why should Rosenhaus care? By then, he was handling more than $100 million in contracts, ranking him among the top agents in football. From where he sat, there was only Steinberg's success to envy.

"He's the king right now," Rosenhaus said of Steinberg. "He's got quarterbacks, he's got more clients than I do, he makes more money than I do. But he's been at it a lot longer than I have. Give me the same amount of time, and I'll blow him out of the water."

4

No Limit

As 1999 turned into 2000, Leigh Steinberg imagined himself as CEO of a nascent sports dynasty. Assante, the financial management company that had purchased Steinberg's firm, had the kind of deep pockets that got him dreaming about an acquisition spree. "I liked this whole idea of being on top of an empire and buying out a lot of agencies in different sports and building out a big marketing arm, a big special-project thing, and then the potential to go gangbusters on charity," Steinberg said. He may have had global ambitions, but he was still a Berkeley liberal whose parents had raised him to care about those who didn't have it as good.

Assante bought a hockey agency and an up-and-coming basketball practice that represented the number-one pick in that year's NBA draft (the University of Cincinnati's

Kenyon Martin). The company also deepened its football practice by purchasing Maximum Sports Management, one of the few black-owned agencies. Maximum represented Emmitt Smith, who ranks first among the NFL's all-time leading rushers, and Curtis Martin, who ranks fifth on that same list. Maximum also represented Rod Woodson and Deion Sanders, two of the best defensive backs to ever wear a uniform. "There seemed to be no limit to what we could achieve," Steinberg said.

Yet Steinberg was hardly the only one thinking about the wealth that could be amassed representing the globe's most famous athletes. The 3 or 4 or 5 percent cut on a contract was only a fraction of the money to be made—almost a loss leader compared to the marketing deals and endorsements and other opportunities that presented themselves in a growing and changing media market. "Consolidation," as academics Kenneth L. Shropshire, Timothy Davis, and N. Jeremi Duru described it in their book, *The Business of Sports Agents*, was fueled by "this belief that sports is a component of the larger entertainment industry."

A year or two before Assante purchased Steinberg's firm, the Interpublic Group, a publicly traded advertising conglomerate, had bought two firms and merged them to form

Octagon, which still ranks among the world's largest sports agencies. SFX became a large player when it spent $100 million to buy the rights to Michael Jordan and the rest of David Falk's basketball practice. So, too, did Wall Street financier Ted Forstmann, who spent $750 million to buy IMG, an agency of long standing that at that time represented Tiger Woods and Roger Federer. Then there was CAA, which already represented many of the most sought-after actors, writers, and directors in Hollywood, and was moving aggressively into sports. In the age of speedy conglomeration, a shakeout seemed inevitable, and the Assante deal fell apart less than four years after it had been consummated.

To this day, Steinberg doesn't quite understand what happened. Maybe it was changes in upper management, he said. Maybe it was a shift in corporate strategy that no one bothered to share with him. What he knew for certain was that he no longer had money to expand his operation. "They lost interest and stopped funding new investments in other firms, as well as our efforts to build a marketing and production company," Steinberg said. Cost cutting followed, which Steinberg and the other agents came to resent. "A lot of people had advised me against selling," Steinberg said, including Patriots owner Robert Kraft. "They told me I was too accustomed to running my own shop. I guess they were right."

While he was still with Assante, Steinberg continued to represent players. Wide receiver Plaxico Burress was one of three first-rounders he represented in the 2000 draft. That same year he picked up veteran running back Ricky Williams. Williams's first contract underscored the notion that there are sometimes good reasons to change agents. Williams, who had won the 1998 Heisman Trophy, was the fifth overall pick in the 1999 draft. He signed with No Limit Sports Management, the fledgling agency rapper Master P had created a year earlier. The agent working on Williams's deal with the Saints had gotten him an $8.8 million signing bonus ("Decent enough," Steinberg declared) but the rest of the seven-year, $68 million package was weighted too heavily toward hard-to-reach incentives. Williams earned only the league minimum during his first two years, when injuries limited his playing time. He was excellent in his third year, when he ran for more than 1,200 yards for the Saints. After being traded to the Dolphins in his fourth year, he was even better, running for nearly 1,900 yards. But he needed to rush for a combined 6,400 yards in his first four years and score a lot more touchdowns for most of the incentive money to kick in, Steinberg said.

"Taking Ricky on was basically a rescue mission"—and also its own odyssey. Williams temporarily retired from football just prior to what would have been his sixth season in the league to become a yoga instructor. He unretired a season later but missed another year due to a drug suspension (for marijuana use). During the eleven years he played in the NFL, Williams rushed for more than ten thousand yards.

But there was more going on in Steinberg's life than a shift in corporate strategy and some meddlesome accountants suddenly looking over his shoulder. Clues that the famed agent might have had a drinking problem predate the sale to Assante. In 1996, he was arrested for drunk driving after attending a charity fundraiser. The next year he made a spectacle of himself at the wedding of one of his star clients, Drew Bledsoe, the starting quarterback for the New England Patriots. It's usually the agent who counsels his players about controlling their alcohol intake when in public, but Steinberg was so inebriated, Bledsoe later testified in court, that friends and family were asking him, "Who the hell is that guy?" Steinberg's drinking would also embarrass him at a party he threw after the Pats won a divisional playoff game (in Bledsoe's telling, Steinberg made a pass at the wife of one of Bledsoe's teammates) and then again at the Pro Bowl in Hawaii, when he made so many visits to the minibar that he "passed out on the deck."

Steinberg was in his second year at Assante when David Dunn, the young agent he had brought into the firm in 1997, and Brian Murphy, another employee, quit to start their own agency. One-third of the Steinberg, Moorad & Dunn staff joined them at their new outfit, Athletes First, which would now represent more than half of Steinberg's football clients, including Bledsoe and future Hall of Fame tight end Tony Gonzalez. Steinberg had left them no choice, Dunn and Murphy testified when the split ended up in an Orange County courtroom. They worked hard to recruit and retain athletes and watched as their famous boss neglected them. "He simply signs them and never sees them again," Murphy said.

Steinberg described himself as "stunned." He seemed particularly hard hit by Dunn's defection. Steinberg had given him his first job as an agent, he said, and looked at him "like a younger brother." Assante sued and won a $44 million verdict against Dunn and Athletes First, but as Steinberg put it, "It's not like I saw any of that money."

Steinberg's personal life brought more stress. He had married in 1985 and was living with his wife and their three kids in their Newport Beach home when a mold problem prompted them to move. They would demolish a second house when the same issue developed there. The couple discovered that first one son and then another had a degenerative eye condition that was likely to leave them blind. "With everything going on," he said, "I turned to alcohol to check out and escape."

Steinberg bought his practice back from Assante in 2003 for $4 million. He hired a few young agents and went back to recruiting players. He was temporarily back on top when one of his agents, Ryan Tollner, established a good rapport with Ben Roethlisberger when he was still a promising college quarterback at Miami University in Ohio (sixteen seasons later, Roethlisberger has two Super Bowl rings and is a certain Hall of Famer), but mainly Steinberg represented lower picks such as Chad Morton, a speedy but undersized (5'8") running back from the University of Southern California whom the Saints took a chance on with a fifth-round pick.

There would be little good news for Steinberg in the coming years. His father, who had been a great influence in his life, died in 2004. Around that same time, Steinberg separated from his wife and moved out of the house. Where once he drank after the kids had gone to sleep, now he drank anytime he wanted. Morton, who carved out a seven-year career as return specialist, sued him. Unbeknownst to Steinberg, a partner in a side venture in China had borrowed $300,000 from Morton—a clear violation of the rules established by the NFL Players Association, which prohibited agents from taking loans from players. "My signature was forged; I didn't know anything about it. I said, 'Okay, instead of three hundred thousand dollars, what if I pay him four hundred thousand?'" Steinberg said. But it was too late; a rival agent reported the violation to the players union. The NFL Players Association requires every agent to pay an annual fee (as of 2020, that was $1,500 for agents representing fewer than ten active players and $2,000 for those with more) to maintain their certification. Seeing what was coming, Steinberg declined renewal and let his junior partners take over representation of their remaining clients until he could clear his name.

An intervention led to a monthlong stay at a chemical dependency center in 2007. One month after that, Steinberg crashed his Mercedes ML 500 into three parked cars and a fire hydrant. His fame ensured that the accident and his subsequent arrest on a DUI charge was national news

("'Jerry Maguire' Agent Arrested for Drunk Driving," blared a typical headline). "I know that it's not acceptable to get behind the wheel after having consumed any amount of alcohol," Steinberg said, sounding like so many of the athletes he had counseled. "I take full responsibility for my behavior, and I will take appropriate action to prevent any remotely similar behavior in the future." Despite his promise, there would be another arrest on a charge of public intoxication, and he would later admit he blacked out while celebrating with Steve Young and his family on the night the 49ers retired the quarterback's jersey.

"I moved into my parents' home, where I spent much of the time consuming bottle after bottle of vodka," he wrote in his memoir. At the height of his fame, Steinberg's drink of choice had been Grey Goose. With time, he started buying cheaper vodkas—Blue Ice, Smirnoff—until eventually he was consuming 1.75-liter plastic jugs of Popov.

DAVID DUNN, THE AGENT who had led the coup against Steinberg while they were all working at Assante, was hit with a two-year suspension by the NFL Players Association for his actions. His new agency, Athletes First, declared

Chapter 11 bankruptcy, and the suspension was put on hold while he appealed the $44 million judgment against him. Meanwhile, he and his partners continued to recruit new clients. Their sales pitch was a team approach that assured athletes that there was always someone on call if they needed them. Among those they signed during this period was quarterback Carson Palmer, who earned more than $170 million during his fifteen years in the NFL, and linebacker Ray Lewis, a Hall of Famer who earned nearly $100 million during his seventeen-year career.

Ultimately, an appellate court threw out the initial verdict against Dunn, and the Players Association reduced its punishment to eighteen months. During that period, Athletes First signed five more first-rounders, including Clay Matthews, the future star linebacker. In 2013, they signed Aaron Rodgers, who five years later became the highest-paid player in the NFL when he signed a four-year, $134 million deal ($100 million of which was guaranteed) with the Packers. In 2018, Dunn managed nearly $850 million in active NFL contracts, according to *Forbes*, which ranked him twenty-fourth on its annual list of top agents.

Those who inherited the remains of Steinberg's practice—an estimated forty clients—fared similarly well. Roethlisberger became the marquee client for a firm that Tollner and his cousin Bruce, who also had worked for Steinberg, called Rep1 Sports. Like their old boss, they represent players at every position but specialize in quarterbacks. In 2016, the Tollners would excite sports blogs when they signed Jared Goff from Cal, the number-one pick in that year's draft, and North Dakota State University's Carson Wentz, who went second.

"At one level, I have a certain amount of pride," Steinberg told me. Athletes First and Rep1 Sports are two of the more successful boutique agencies representing NFL players, and even Mike Sullivan represented his share of first-round draft picks before going to work in the front office of the Denver Broncos. "I trained them all," Steinberg said. "To the extent they're doing good things in the world, that's good." He compared himself to the aging head coach who can look across the NFL and see acolytes walking the league's sidelines. "The fact that they can't acknowledge what they got in the relationship isn't my problem," he said.

DON YEE CONTINUED SIGNING less-touted players who nevertheless enjoyed long, prosperous careers in the NFL.

At some point, Yee started representing coaches, and includes the Saints' Sean Payton among his clients. Yet it's his most famous client who continues to be his best earner.

Tom Brady's first deal with the Patriots was hardly a blockbuster. He was a sixth-round pick, and was paid accordingly. He might have gotten a small bonus because he was a quarterback, but if so, pity the underpaid guards and tackles in the same draft slot around that time. Brady received a signing bonus of $38,500 and was paid $193,000 for the year—the league minimum. He took over as the Patriots' starting quarterback in 2002, his second year in the league (replacing former Steinberg client Drew Bledsoe). That same year, he brought New England its first Super Bowl victory. Brady, who was the game's MVP, still had another year on his contract, but Yee was able to negotiate a new contract: a five-year, $30.5 million deal that included a $10 million signing bonus.

Brady led the Patriots to another Super Bowl championship in 2004, and was again named the game's MVP. Once again Yee secured a big raise for his star client, despite there being two years left on his contract. The deal Brady signed a few months after his second Super Bowl victory was a six-year, $60.5 million pact that paid him $26.5 million in bonuses on top of a salary that averaged more than $5 million a year. There would be more Super Bowl appearances and another contract extension. The four-year, $72 million deal Yee hammered out in 2010 was, briefly, the largest in NFL history.

The contract extension Yee negotiated for Brady in 2013, however, proved controversial. He had been named league MVP in both 2007 and 2010. He had brought the Patriots to the Super Bowl in 2008 and again in 2012 (both losses to the New York Giants). Yet the three-year, $27 million deal Yee negotiated was well below the market rate for a quarterback of Brady's caliber. "Already, I hear the whispers and the charges that Yee made a bad deal: what in God's name is he doing signing Brady for such a relative pittance," wrote *Sports Illustrated*'s Peter King. Fellow agents no doubt used the contract against Yee when competing for future clients. But Yee's job was to represent Brady, who wanted the Patriots to have the money to lure other stars to the team. "The thing I have admired about Yee," King wrote, "is that he doesn't care what other people think. He cares about what his client thinks."

There would be another contract in 2016 (a two-year, $41 million extension that included a $28 million signing bonus) and also the contract Brady signed on his forty-second birthday: $23 million for the 2019 season, $30 million in 2020, and $32 million in 2021. Yet even the seemingly immortal Brady learned that, in football, the money is only guaranteed if a team wants to continue paying you. In March of 2020, the future Hall of Famer signed a two-year deal with the Buccaneers worth $50 million. Even if Brady earns the additional $9 million in incentives built into the contracts, that's still several million dollars short of his $62 million deal with the Pats.

Rival agents took on investors, which allowed them to compete with the bigger firms. With that money, they could hire financial services and dedicated PR people, which allowed them to promote themselves as full-service outfits. Yee, however, deliberately kept things small at his firm, Yee & Dubin Sports.

"We generally try to keep it to twenty-five, thirty players," he said, along with around two dozen coaches. Yee and another lawyer represent the coaches, while another three lawyers, all of whom are certified NFL agents (the partner representing coaches doesn't need special certification), work with the players. If Yee and his partners have a bias, it has been toward more serious-minded clients who are willing and able to follow the plans devised for them. "It seems like they go after a certain type of player," said Scott Fujita, a former fifth-round pick who played eleven years as linebacker. "Their expectations for you as a player are very, very simple: act like a pro and do your job." In an interview for a profile of Yee in the University of Virginia's alumni magazine, Fujita added that he had played for four teams, and "No matter who was that team's general manager . . . they always pulled me aside and told me how much they enjoyed working with Don Yee over the years," he said.

"Some of what it means to be a good agent is to do your research before approaching a player and find out who this person is," Yee said. During the recruiting process, he aspires to understand a player's background and some of the personal challenges that athlete has faced, no matter how successful he's been. "The vast majority of players I've encountered have never really had anybody to listen to them," he said. The outside world sees their athletic ability but not the human inside the uniform. All of us are on a journey,

Yee said. The key to connecting with a player is understanding theirs without judgment and with an open mind.

Over breakfast, Yee told me about Pat Tyrance, a favorite client of his, though he earned Yee's agency very little in commissions. Tyrance was an All-American linebacker at the University of Nebraska and the 201st pick in the 1991 draft. He was also accepted into Harvard Medical School. He deferred admission for a year, but after one season in the NFL, chose med school over football. Citing attorney-client privilege, Yee said he couldn't get into the specifics of any conversations they had, but it was obvious to both of them that Tyrance wasn't likely going to be a starter. "You can make a career out of that, obviously, but every year is tenuous. Very hard to plan," Yee said. Today Tyrance is a successful orthopedic surgeon in Hollywood, Florida. "This job is about helping another human being reach his dreams—whatever those are," Yee said.

Yee is an outlier as an agent. He calls himself an "anomaly." He doesn't like being around sports people, and says that the more successfully someone can remove themselves from the sport they play, the better off they probably are. "You'll be far more effective from day one if you dispense with any romantic notions about sports," he said.

He's driven by the pursuit of excellence rather than money or any thrill that comes from being a part of pro sports. "It's about being around people who want to achieve excellence in sports and doing what I can to help make that happen," he said. He describes himself as a student of psychology who does whatever he can to help the athletes to whom he's committed. "I like to think of him as a little Zen master," Julian Edelman said of Yee in an interview with a Boston-area television station in 2017. "It's like *Crouching Tiger, Hidden Dragon*–type stuff. He keeps my mind right." It was a compliment, even though it might come across as condescending and racially tinged.

"We spend a lot of time trying to train the players psychologically," Yee said, "to develop a strong mental protocol in how they approach the job—whether that's rehabbing from an injury, studying the playbook, working on techniques related to their particular positions, communicating with their coaches, or staying disciplined to whatever financial plan their [adviser] has laid out for them. We try to get them to understand that this type of emotional and psychological discipline will enhance their actual performance."

Unlike Steinberg and Rosenhaus, Yee prefers life outside

the media's eye. Yet serving a client, Yee learned, sometimes meant standing in the spotlight on behalf of a player, as he's done numerous times for Tom Brady, who is similarly media-shy. It was Yee who put out a statement in 2007 when gossip columns were reporting that Brady, who was already dating supermodel Gisele Bündchen, had impregnated his ex-girlfriend, the actress Bridget Moynahan. ("Tom and his family are excited about the pregnancy, and want to thank everyone who has shown support, and particularly for their consideration of Tom's privacy," Yee wrote in a statement he gave to the Associated Press.) Yee was more front and center when Deflategate hit and the NFL learned of the alleged deflation of the balls used in the 2015 AFC championship game, played at home in New England. A report commissioned by the league charged that Brady was "probably" aware that the balls had been deflated. Yee went on MSNBC to call the verdict a "terrible disappointment." In an interview with CBSSports.com, he dismissed the report as based on "junk" science.

"Part of the job of an agent is fighting for your clients," Yee said. "It's about being their advocate and putting forward their point of view." If Yee is out there, that means Brady doesn't have to be.

———

ANOTHER AGENT MIGHT HAVE felt humiliated. But Drew Rosenhaus was no ordinary agent. The *Sports Illustrated* article was devastating. It depicted Rosenhaus as bombastic and crude, a loud egomaniac who was like a toxin infecting the game. The "dark knight" of football, as *SI* dubbed him. Worse, the article also made clear that he wasn't necessarily the genius he imagined himself to be. He was a gambler who would always have another chance at a big payoff, even if his client would not.

Naturally, Rosenhaus exulted in the notoriety. Proving the old adage that no publicity is bad publicity, he screamed from the rooftops that he was the first agent *Sports Illustrated* had ever put on its cover. (He remained the one and only until 2019, when the magazine published a cover story about basketball agent Rich Paul.) Not even Steinberg made the cover, despite all his quarterbacks.

The magazine became a prop in Rosenhaus's practice. When a star receiver for the Miami Hurricanes stopped returning his calls in 1997, Rosenhaus and his brother drove six hours to his hometown. At just the right moment, Rosenhaus pulled out the magazine. The cover was a tight close-up of his face looking intense (if not angry) overlaid with these words in bold letters: "I am a ruthless warrior. I am a hit man. I will move in for the kill and use everything within my power to succeed for my clients." That was his sales pitch: someone who will do anything to help the client come out ahead in a deal. "Can't you see how I will annihilate anyone who gets in our way?" he told recruits. "Can't you see that, as a team, we can't be beat?"

Leigh Steinberg boasted so often about being the model for Jerry Maguire that Tom Cruise attempted to publicly shame him into shutting up about it. ("It got to the point where it was a little ridiculous," the actor told HBO in 2002.) Rosenhaus similarly bragged about his connection to the movie that shaped the world's understanding of their business. Cameron Crowe had spent some time with Rosenhaus when researching the movie, and even gave him a cameo. Yet Rosenhaus seemed oblivious to the obvious—or maybe just immune to it—when he bragged about his role in shaping the film: he's the model for Bob Sugar, the bottom-feeder and scoundrel everyone who watches the movie roots against.

But Rosenhaus was selling something players were eager to buy. He picked up star receiver Plaxico Burress after Steinberg's career crashed and burned, and also took over representation of running back Edgerrin James, who ranks thirteenth on the NFL's all-time rushing list. By the mid-2000s, Rosenhaus represented ninety-one players in the NFL—tops in the league, and as many as Steinberg represented at his peak. Rosenhaus Sports Entertainment also picked up running back Frank Gore, third on the all-time rushing list, and Rob Gronkowski, the Patriots' dominant tight end.

Yet Terrell Owens was probably the best offensive player Rosenhaus ever represented. (Warren Sapp was his best defensive player.) Owens—or T.O., as he liked to be called—ranks third all-time in receiving yardage and fifth in touchdowns. He was fantastic on the 49ers, where he played for the first eight years of his career before eventually wearing out his welcome, and was equally amazing in his first year with the Eagles, his next team. The Eagles made the Super Bowl that year, and Owens, though he'd broken his leg and torn a ligament seven weeks earlier and had been warned not to play, led both teams with nine receptions for 122 yards.

Owens had every reason to dump his first agent. Because of a missed deadline, he had been deemed ineligible for free agency, though obviously he wanted out of San Francisco. The 49ers traded him to the Ravens, but Owens refused to go. He said he wanted to play for the Philadelphia Eagles; so, to clean up the mess, the league arranged a deal for Owens to sign a seven-year, $49 million contract with Philly. A few months after the Super Bowl, Owens signed on with Rosenhaus, who argued that T.O. deserved a raise, given his big-game heroics. He was already outperforming his contract, Rosenhaus said.

The problem with the strategy of telling an athlete that a team is underpaying him is that it breeds resentment. The Eagles' front office declined to renegotiate one year into a seven-year deal, and the wider world watched Owens openly feud with his quarterback and coaches. Seven weeks into the season, Philadelphia suspended Owens for the rest of the year, a punishment that cost the receiver just under $2.5 million in lost wages. "Instead of getting my client a new deal, he lost a fortune, was suspended, and saw his season come to an end," Rosenhaus admitted.

Owens was so good that he continued to thrive despite the lost year and his reputation as a difficult player. He had signed a seven-year deal with the Eagles, but the team gave him an unconditional release, freeing Rosenhaus to negotiate with any other team. This time Owens signed a more typical three-year deal with the Cowboys that paid him $34.7 million over that period, instead of the $20 million he would have been paid had he stayed with the Eagles. Owens was great with the Cowboys, but he again wore out his welcome, and there would be no contract extension or new deal. Once again, Rosenhaus put Owens up for bidding. T.O. then signed consecutive one-year deals with the Bills (for $6.3 million) and the Bengals (for $3.2 million).

Ultimately, Owens felt ripped off by Rosenhaus and his brother. Almost all of the $80 million he had been paid for playing in the NFL was gone, Owens confessed in an interview with *GQ*, and it was the Rosenhauses who had introduced Owens to his financial adviser, a man who ended up being banned from the securities industry in part because of his role in persuading thirty-one NFLers to invest in an Alabama casino. (The project went bankrupt, costing the group an estimated $40 million.) Owens sued the Rosenhauses, alleging that he lost more than $5 million entrusting his money to the financial adviser.

An agent's job is to steer clients away from people like this adviser, who had previously been accused of stealing from his clients. Instead, Owens's lawyer claimed, Rosenhaus pushed Owens toward him. The suit was dismissed, however, and Owens became just another footballer who earned crazy amounts of money yet had little to show for it. At the end of 2019, T.O. was reportedly worth $100,000.

5

Dandy

Tory Dandy didn't know what a sports agent did until he was about to meet one. He was a junior at Tusculum University in Tennessee, and a friend, a football standout, was hearing from people interested in representing him. "This friend didn't have much in the way of family support, so he asked me to help him," Dandy said, adding, "The blind leading the blind."

Dandy grew up in a small town in South Carolina, raised by a single mother who was always "hustling and bustling," he said, to provide for him and his two older sisters. He was in his twenties when he met his father for the first time. His mother worked as a nurse's aide at a local hospital and cared for patients on the side and took cleaning jobs around town to earn extra money. Her youngest was a good student but an even better athlete who excelled at track and football. He made All-Region as a wide receiver on his high school team, earning him a full scholarship to play for Tusculum.

But a torn hamstring Dandy suffered in high school never fully healed, and by his junior year he had torn muscles in both shoulders, ending his career. "You always have aspirations of playing in the NFL and all that," he said. "Who knows what would've happened?" If nothing else, the experience of seeing his dreams dashed at so young an age gave him an abiding respect for anyone who did make it. Dandy understood what it meant to go through two-a-days and to practice so hard that you wanted to puke and to absorb hits that left your head ringing for days. "I have a high-level respect for anyone who makes the NFL and how hard they worked to get there," he said.

Unlike some former athletes, Dandy expresses no bitterness toward the game. For starters, it paid for his college education. He earned a degree in business with a minor in sports management. "I had always focused on my academics," he said. "I wasn't relying on football." His mother had six brothers and sisters, his father eighteen siblings. "I'm the first person in my family to go to college and finish," he said.

While still in school, Dandy imagined that he might become a coach or find a job with a college sports program. "I thought I was going to be an athletic director somewhere," he said. Then he helped his teammate and friend choose Synergy Sports Inc. to represent him. The friend never made it in the NFL, but the experience led to Dandy's big break: an internship with Synergy while working on his MBA at Webster University, just outside St. Louis.

"Coming from a single-parent home," Dandy said, "never seeing your father." He himself had fathered a child while he was still in high school. "Having a daughter in the tenth grade," he continued. "Many say you're not supposed to ever make it out."

SYNERGY COULDN'T COMPETE WITH a Steinberg or a Rosenhaus in its representation of big-name stars, but it had its share of moneymakers when Dandy worked there in the early 2000s. Richard Seymour, who played in seven Pro

Bowls and won three Super Bowls with New England, was a client, as was John Abraham, twice a first-team All-Pro who played in the NFL for fifteen years. Synergy was what Dandy called a "small boutique firm," with twenty to thirty clients. Synergy hired him as its director of recruiting after he graduated from business school, which meant Dandy would help the firm identify college players to pursue and travel to colleges to make first contact. But then Synergy imploded only a few months after he had started working there full-time. The two founders weren't "seeing eye-to-eye," Dandy said, and suddenly he was out of a job.

"I was devastated," said Dandy, who was then twenty-four years old. "I'm from small-town South Carolina. I didn't have any resources. I barely knew anyone in this industry. I was thinking, 'How do I get back in?'"

Part of what it means to work for a sports agency is knowing the names of the competition. "For me, I wanted to see who the top African American agents were," he said. He kept coming across the same name: Eugene Parker. Parker and Roosevelt Barnes Jr. cofounded Maximum Sports Management, the agency that Assante briefly owned during Leigh Steinberg's ill-fated tenure as an executive there.

Dandy had met Parker while he was still an intern at Synergy. "He was speaking at this conference, so I just walked up to him, introduced myself, and told him I admired him. I then kind of asked for some pointers," he said. The two spoke for maybe fifteen or twenty minutes. After that, Dandy would drop Parker the occasional e-mail or give him a call, "just to keep in touch and remind him I was out there," he said.

Dandy reached out to Parker after losing his job at Synergy. A couple of months later, Parker was in Atlanta, and Dandy went to see him. Parker reminded Dandy of something he had told him: in this business, you have your name and little else. An underling's misdeed could do serious damage to a person's reputation, as Leigh Steinberg was learning around this same time after one of his people took a loan from a client. "He told me, 'I'm very cautious about who I allow to use my name, who I partner with,'" Dandy said. "But then he said, 'There's something about you. I want to give you the opportunity.' And he did." A few months after Dandy had lost his job, Parker hired him as Maximum's director of recruiting. Parker took Dandy with him when he and Barnes sold Maximum to Relativity Sports in 2013. "Eugene and I worked together for almost twelve years," Dandy said.

Emmitt Smith had retired a couple of years before Dandy joined Parker and Barnes at Maximum Sports, as had two more future Hall of Famers, Deion Sanders and Rod Woodson. But Maximum still had Hines Ward, who had been named Super Bowl MVP in 2006, and Larry Fitzgerald, who was only a few years into an amazing career that took him to number two on the all-time receiving yards list, on its roster. It was Dandy's job to ensure that the firm had a future by recruiting more top talent.

"The guys we've typically worked with over the years, they're the first in their families to graduate from college, they're the first ones with any kind of money," Barnes said. That was Barnes's and Parker's experience, and also Dandy's, which he used to sell himself and the agency to prospective recruits.

Occasionally Dandy also handled client maintenance; that was life at a smaller firm that employed only five or six people. But the bulk of his job entailed doing what he described as "groundwork": "That can be evaluation of players—who we should recruit, how to reach those people—and then going out and establishing relations," he said. The first two clients he recruited to the firm were University of Tennessee football players he met through a cousin.

"Gene [Eugene Parker] flew in as the closer," Dandy said.

"He negotiated the contracts. But I was the point person for making the deal happen." Two years later, Dandy hit it big when he signed Louisiana State University's Tyson Jackson, considered the best defensive lineman in that year's draft. Dandy was only twenty-nine years old, but his hard work meant that Maximum represented the number-three overall pick in the 2009 draft. Jackson never became the star some expected him to be, but his first contract paid him $57 million over five years, and the next one was a five-year, $25 million deal that included roughly $12 million guaranteed. Recruiting Jackson brought in over $2 million in fees.

Gene Parker proved an ideal mentor. "It was his character," Dandy said. "His integrity. His genuineness and how much he cared for his clients." Parker died from kidney cancer in 2016 when he was only sixty years old, and the obituaries made him out to be larger-than-life. *USA Today* described Parker as a "titan and pioneer," and Liz Mullen, who since 1998 has written a weekly column about agents for the *Sports Business Journal*, remembered him as "charismatic, brilliant, and innovative." In the obituary she wrote, Mullen highlighted Parker's skill as an agent. She reminded readers of the deal he negotiated with the Cowboys for

Deion Sanders, a seven-year, $35 million pact that included a record $13 million signing bonus. The front-loading of so much of the money—no small feat in a sport where the rest of a contract is dependent on a player's remaining on the roster—impressed Mullen, as did the way the bonus was spread out over seven years so that not all $13 million would count toward that year's salary cap. "Soon after, the NFL and the NFL Players Association negotiated what is called the 'Deion Rule,'" Mullen wrote, "to stop clubs and agents from ever doing it again."

Dandy learned about recruiting from Parker, starting with the importance of listening and patience. He learned the nuances of negotiating a deal, and Parker's catchphrase became his own: "The same you recruit 'em, you got to keep them." Too many agents promise the world when they're courting a prospect but then are too busy wooing the next set of recruits to deliver. "I tell my families all the time, 'I'll put down my phone and you can call any client I have, or their family, and ask them, whether they were a first-round pick or a seventh-round pick, is Tory Dandy part of your life?' And the answer from all of them will be yes. I'm in for the long haul, through good and bad," Dandy said. With pride, he told me about a client, a wide receiver, who was projected to be a first-round draft choice until he broke his leg so badly that a rod had to be inserted. He could risk fighting for a roster spot as a lower-round draft choice, but if he did, he would forfeit a disability policy that would pay him $2 million tax free.

"That was a hard conversation that involved a lot of crying and praying," Dandy said. "He would give up the sport he grew up loving."

Parker proved to be more than just an experienced hand who could teach Dandy the finer points of being a quality representative. "Really what it was for me is what Eugene stood for as a man," Dandy said. The boy who grew up without a father had found a stand-in with Parker. "Eugene was a father figure for me," he said. "I learned a lot of life lessons outside the business." It was under Parker's guidance that Dandy prepared himself for his certification, which meant writing a $2,500 nonrefundable check and taking a proctored, sixty-question exam. "Eugene told me I was ready," Dandy said, but he waited another year or two. "I wanted to sharpen the iron before jumping out there," he said. "I was still learning."

Dandy had been certified for several years and was building his own client base when Parker was diagnosed with a fast-moving form of kidney cancer in 2016. Dandy's contract with Relativity expired that same year. As word spread inside the provincial world of sports agents that an accomplished African American agent was available, Dandy heard from a lot of firms. He met with only a few, however. "I was very cautious in thinking where I wanted to go next," he said.

By that time, CAA had emerged as the industry's new colossus. Its big move into football had come in 2006, when it bought the football practice of superagent Tom Condon, a former offensive lineman who represented marquee clients, including the Manning brothers. "The firm that represented Tom Cruise and Angelina Jolie," *Sports Illustrated* wrote when reporting the news, "joined forces with the guy who represented Peyton and Eli Manning." Over the next decade, Condon brought in rivals Jimmy Sexton and Todd France, whose firm, Five Star Athlete Management, represented roughly fifty NFL players. The firm's current list of clients includes Drew Brees, Matthew Stafford, Matt Ryan, and Julio Jones, among other stars. The firm dominates *Forbes*'s annual list of agents so thoroughly that it's no longer a contest, at least in football. In 2019, the commissions they earned ranked France and Condon first and second among football agents, while Sexton ranked fifth. CAA had $4.3 billion in contracts under management that year, more than twice that of its nearest competitor. It also ranked first in basketball with $2.3 billion in contracts, second in hockey, and third in baseball.

The news that Dandy was joining CAA hit the wires in the middle of 2016. "Overall, CAA had the total package," he explained. "They had a platform. They had the resources. They had the relationships. They had the back office. So I felt for myself, and more so for my clients, [that] if I had a great situation, they had a great situation." I teased him about joining the giant eating the rest of the industry, but Dandy said he didn't look at it that way. The firm had set him up in his own office in Charlotte, North Carolina, and hired support staff to help him. It felt like having his own practice, even though he's part of a much larger organization. He bounces ideas off his senior colleagues, and they sometimes bounce ideas off him.

"If I'm thinking I want to get sixteen million dollars for you as a wide receiver, I'm not asking anyone, 'Should I ask for sixteen million?'" Dandy said. "That's what I believe through my experience and knowing the game. I determine what I want to get for my clients."

———

THE FIRST TIME I met with Dandy was in the summer of 2019, when he was in New Jersey to sign veteran Giants linebacker Markus Golden. Several months earlier, Dandy had heard that Golden had fired his agent. He was considering his approach when Golden reached out to him. "He knew somebody that I knew, and they connected us," he said. He immediately flew to New Jersey to talk with Golden. "He told me he wanted to take his time," Dandy said. "I kept in touch with him periodically." Golden phoned to give him the good news, and Dandy came to New Jersey to get his signature on a contract. He laughed when I asked why he didn't just take care of the paperwork via FedEx or a document review app.

"You always do it face-to-face," he said. "You can't say you're taking charge of someone's career and leading and guiding them through this process but, you know what, we'll send you the contract."

Dandy walked me through his basic pitch. I imagined him leading with CAA and the many stars it represents, but he sells mainly himself. "Honestly, a guy isn't going to care that another agent at CAA has this big star or the other," he said. "A guy has to feel and understand that if you're the one leading them in their career, you have the competence to get the job done."

Contract negotiations are largely formulaic and, thanks to the NFL's slotting system, depend on where in the draft a player was taken. Dandy negotiated a four-year, $29.16 million contract for Denzel Ward, the number-four pick in 2018, which was slightly above the amount paid to the number-five pick but slightly less than the number three. A year later, he secured a four-year, $29.32 million deal for Devin White, the number-five pick in the 2019 draft. The $19.29 million signing bonus he secured for Ward in 2018 was, one year later, a $19.34 million bonus for a number-five pick. The first twenty-four selections in the 2019 draft received guaranteed contracts (there seems to be no rational reason that the line is there instead of on the thirty-second and last pick of the first round except that that's where the line has been for the last several years), which meant that most of Dandy's clients would not get guaranteed money. As Dandy is forever explaining to the families and players he recruits, each contract has its "layers." The signing bonus, as the name implies, is paid when an athlete inks his name on a deal. But the rest of the contract depends on a player's making the roster each year. Oshane Ximines received a signing bonus of $836,780 (payments were spread over four years for cap reasons) and earned the basic rookie salary of $495,000 in year one of his contract. Ximines is slated to make $618,000 in his second year, $707,00 in his third, and $796,000 in his fourth—unless his team, the New York Giants, decides he's not worth that money and drops him before one of the deadlines specified in the contract. That's reality in a league where salaries aren't guaranteed, and it can make players feel discarded after years of adulation.

"Beneath it all, they're young men going through the same things we all go through," Dandy said. "Except a lot of the time they don't have people to check on them. 'Okay, what's going on with you behind everything else?' They've got this platform, but there's a lot of pressure that goes along with that platform." It's their agent who can serve as both sounding board and release valve for young athletes who know their every public utterance will be scrutinized.

Dandy described himself as having a "very hands-on approach" to client maintenance, but nearly every agent says that. His main pitch is invariably the tale of his improbable journey from teenage father in a broken home to the living room chair or kitchen table where he's currently sitting. He targets players who grew up in similar circumstances and might appreciate an agent who shares that upbringing. "In my experience, these guys are going to go with people they're comfortable with," he said.

Dandy stressed that he's always listening when recruiting. "I need to get an understanding of their wants and needs and desires," he said. "I need to understand who they are." That helps him create a connection and also lets him weigh his feelings about a prospect. Some players look for a valida-tor, a yes-man. "That's not me," he said. He's also not the agent to tell them they're the best, as some athletes want.

"I'm not trying to represent every player," he said. "Every player is not a fit for me. I'm not a fit for every player."

6

The Comeback

L eigh Steinberg took his last drink in 2010. Two years later, he filed for bankruptcy. From the outside, it was hard to fathom: an individual once worth $75 million was, a decade later, broke. Steinberg cited his divorce and the millions he'd donated to charity when he was flush. He spent $7 million on the Steinberg Leadership Institute, a training program aimed at fighting the spread of racism and anti-Semitism in the United States. "I wasn't alive during the Holocaust, but this is my watch," he explained. With the rise of white supremacist groups in the 1990s and 2000s, he said, "I couldn't just sit there and not do something." He made millions on a sports-related e-commerce app he helped develop, but also lost what he described as a "fortune" gambling on Internet stocks at the end of the 1990s.

Steinberg secured his recertification from the NFL

Players Association in 2013. That same year he launched a new agency, Steinberg Sports & Entertainment. His plan was to sign a big-name athlete who would make a splash and herald his return. But first he needed money to set up an office and to fly around the country in search of the client who would put him back on top. Despite the adverse publicity his downfall had sparked, he said, "there were all sorts of people wanting to invest in my new firm, thinking [it] could be a successful thing on the cheap." He ended up securing funding from a group in Houston. "They were in the oil business but were nuts about football," Steinberg said. They also liked the numbers. The NFL was on pace to book $12 billion in revenue in 2014—nearly double the amount made just a decade earlier. The league was also setting viewership records: nineteen of the twenty most-watched television shows in US history were football games. Player salaries continued to rise, and with them the commissions agents could charge. And, of course, there was the money to be made on the marketing deals that the NFL's biggest stars would command.

Steinberg's first year back was rough. His sole client in the 2014 draft was a quarterback who was picked in the sixth round and then cut before the season even started. Two years later, Paxton Lynch was supposed to resurrect Steinberg's career. "Potential 1st overall pick," Steinberg tweeted out when announcing that he had signed Lynch. It didn't quite turn out that way, but the Denver Broncos took Lynch with the twenty-sixth pick in the 2016 draft to replace Peyton Manning, who had just announced his retirement. Lynch made the cover of *Sports Illustrated*, and Steinberg earned more than $150,000 in fees on Lynch's $5.1 million signing bonus. But the Broncos' heir apparent would last all of two seasons with the team.

Few seemed to think Steinberg had found his savior when he signed Texas Tech University's Patrick Mahomes ahead of the 2017 draft. The touts and draft kings rated several quarterbacks above Mahomes and expected him to go in the second round or later. Scouts questioned Mahomes's unorthodox throwing style and expressed doubts about his ability to transition to the pro game after running the freewheeling "air raid" offense Texas Tech played. "People thought, 'He's a gunslinger. Undisciplined,'" Steinberg said. "What they missed is that he was a freakishly gifted athlete with the ability to run a complicated offense."

Steinberg had no ties to Texas Tech but used his connections to get a phone number for the family. The young quarterback was going into his junior year the first time

Steinberg and Chris Cabott, a young lawyer he had taken on as a partner, flew to Texas to meet with Mahomes's parents. There was a second visit with the parents before Steinberg first met Mahomes himself—and that was only a quick hello after the game he and Cabott attended with the Mahomes family. The quarterback's father, Patrick Mahomes Sr., had been a major league pitcher for eleven years. Mahomes's stepfather, LaTroy Hawkins, had pitched in the majors for twenty-one years. "The family was really taking their time," Steinberg said.

Liz Mullen, the *Sports Business Journal* columnist, heard regularly from Steinberg. "He'd call me every year saying it's time for me to write his comeback story," she said. He called at the start of 2017 to talk about Mahomes. "He's telling me he's signed this kid, he's a first-round pick," she said. That wasn't what she was hearing, so she sat on the story until another agent told her about the seventy-eight-yard pass Mahomes had thrown on his pro day at Texas Tech. (A pro day workout is when a college team hosts scouts and executives from around the NFL who are interested in seeing any of their athletes play.) Two weeks before the draft, Mullen finally gave Steinberg the article he wanted under the headline, "Steinberg Client Mahomes Is Moving Up in

Draft Projections." The former Red Raider wound up being the tenth pick of the draft that year.

Mahomes barely played his rookie year. He opened his second season in the NFL by throwing ten touchdowns in his first two starts—an NFL record. He threw for more than five thousand yards and fifty touchdowns that year, tied for the second most in NFL history. He was named the league's MVP and struck deals with Adidas, Proctor & Gamble, and insurance company State Farm. "Paxton Lynch was my breakthrough, telling everyone I was back," Steinberg said. "But Mahomes cemented it. The hottest player in pro football." After leading the Chiefs to victory in Super Bowl LIV in 2020, Mahomes was named the game's MVP, giving Steinberg arguably the top player in all of football.

STEINBERG SPORTS & ENTERTAINMENT occupies a second-floor office in a building on the harbor in Newport

Beach. Thirteen people worked there at the end of 2019, including four certified agents, a vice president of social media, a VP of media relations, and two interns. The dress code was sports-agent casual: Hawaiian shirts, short-sleeved polos, shorts.

By that point, Steinberg Sports represented around twenty-five NFL players, but Steinberg, who'd celebrated his seventieth birthday earlier in the year, was never the kind to stand pat when he saw new territories to conquer. He decided to move into basketball and baseball starting in 2020. He brought up other areas he was exploring with me, including investing in a performance-enhancing sports drink and an app aimed at stadium-goers. For years he's been hosting the Agent Academy, a daylong seminar marketed to people who are serious about becoming agents, and an event he calls the Leigh Steinberg Sports Career Conference.

Steinberg is a born lecturer who seems to love nothing more than pontificating on the sports agent's life. "Being an agent has three components to it," he said shortly after I settled into a chair across from his desk. He leaned back and, propping up a foot, began: "The first is recruiting." Get to know the assistant coaches, he counseled, who invariably will know the names of those who serve as a particular athlete's Praetorian Guard. "To recruit someone, it might take a village. It's maybe the pastor, it may be the brother-in-law, it may be the coach," Steinberg said. "It requires laying all these seeds down." Be prepared for a grilling. Families these days are often armed with a battery of questions they've gotten from the NFL Players Association.

"The most important skill in all this isn't your [power] of persuasion. It's listening," Steinberg said. "If I can peel back the layers of the onion and understand their deepest anxieties and fears, and their greatest hopes and dreams, that's the formula for fulfilling them." He runs recruits through an exercise that explores preferences in everything from proximity to family and weather to long-term economic goals and risk tolerance. "The essence of recruiting is putting yourself in the heart and mind of another human being and seeing the world the way they see it," he said.

At Steinberg's shop, agents create a booklet for every athlete on their target lists. The most important element, Steinberg said, is what they call a "path to the draft"—a detailed, step-by-step guide to what they'll do to improve an athlete's stock. "I find that athletes, because their lives are very structured, feel more secure if there's a schedule for them to follow," Steinberg said. There's the combine, multiple all-star games for seniors, and pro days. "There are no rules in this process," Steinberg said. A player can decide he's doing all of it, or he could decide to do none of it. "That's the first conversation we're having once someone has chosen us as an agent," he said. Whatever the decision, it'll be the agent who picks up the tab.

Steinberg works the phones in the days leading up to the draft, talking up clients and reaching out to GMs and other front-office decision makers. He's made it his business to study the rosters of every team and to know whether they might need the players he represents. To help raise an athlete's profile, he brings them to the Super Bowl, where they can mingle at the annual bash he's thrown for more than twenty-five years. "Marketing is another aspect of the job at this point," Steinberg said. "We'll design a website for someone; we'll help them with social media." Anything to bang the drum on behalf of a client ahead of the draft.

Contract negotiation is the second component of the job, as Steinberg explained it. He dubbed this phase "billionaires versus millionaires." He bemoaned the lack of "creativity" in a system where salaries are predetermined by draft slot and said his hosannas for the death of contract incentives based on performance targets such as yardage gained or touchdowns scored, which were far more prevalent years ago. (Teams need predictable salaries in a world of salary caps, and incentives introduce an X factor into the equation.) Steinberg spoke of the two general styles of negotiating: the high-concept air battle he wages versus the slow, ground-game approach of a Jeff Moorad, his old partner. Steinberg is always crafting a narrative around data points while positioning an athlete for tomorrow.

One lesson that Steinberg has learned the hard way is to never negotiate a deal in the media. (Drew Rosenhaus said the same thing.) "If you push a proud man against the wall, you create deadlock, and deadlock is anathema to this process," Steinberg said. He also learned through trial and error that, when a deal is done, one should be modest. "Never puff or brag about the contract you just negotiated," he said, "because you're dealing with billionaires, and you've got to show them how this is a win for them."

The third and final component of the job is client care. "Client maintenance is all the day-to-day needs of the client," he explained. Maybe they're angry because they're not getting the playing time they think they deserve; maybe they don't like the coach. "We're the release valve," he said. Better that a player grouses to his agent than to someone who might repeat it to the wrong person. The job has also required him to learn his share of physiology. "How the ankle, knee, shoulder, hip, and back work, what ligaments are, so you're able to give a player advice when they're injured," said Steinberg, who instructs his clients to make him their first phone call after learning they're injured.

Steinberg jumped when I asked what advice he might give to someone interested in breaking into the field. "I'm only asked that question, like, fifty times a day." His first suggestion: study psychology. "Everything in life comes down to relationships between people," he said. Understand what motivates people and be able to predict how they might react, "and you'll be able to navigate your way through this job more gracefully. Psychology is critical to recruiting. It's a critical part of client maintenance. It's critical to negotiating. It's critical everywhere." He also suggested that a would-be agent have a repertoire beyond sports. "Learn to talk about a range of topics, like pop culture and politics and businesses to develop," he said. "Knowing the world of sports is not enough."

Hone your listening skills, Steinberg recommended— no easy task today, when being present in the moment is almost a seditious concept. "Don't look at your phone or worry about what you have to do next or what happened yesterday," he said. "Centralize every bit of focus you have into the meeting that's taking place in the moment."

Steinberg also talked about the perennial value of networking, and suggested carving out a niche to help brand yourself. If you're a lawyer or an accountant who knows about taxes, write an article about taxation rates for athletes. If immigration is your specialty, write a column aimed at helping athletes from outside the United States. "The fact that you're not yet in the field doesn't stop you from picking out some small subset of it and establishing yourself as an expert," he said. "If you understand Title Nine, write an article on that and become the go-to person on that. Whatever the niche is."

Finally, Steinberg recommended internships: intern for a team, a league, a conference, an athletic department, a sports marketing company, an agency. "Get inside an organization, and then get into the mind of your supervisor," he suggested. "And then figure out how to enhance that person's life and make yourself irreplaceable." Stay late: "It'll be eight o'clock and everybody else is gone, so I turn to you because I need help," he said. "And like that, you can make a good impression."

The hard part is getting the job. "People don't hire a whole lot in sports; they don't have some regular recruiting thing," he acknowledged, "so distinguish yourself from the great mass of people out there." One applicant for an internship at his shop sent him a mock-up of an issue of *Sports Illustrated*. "It looked just like *SI*—their font, everything—except it was this young man on the cover and we're announcing we hired him." Every article inside explained how he would enhance the firm.

A second applicant had attended a talk Steinberg gave at Baylor University in Waco, Texas, where he mentioned that he drank so much Diet Dr Pepper that he felt obliged to visit the Dr Pepper Museum while in town. Two weeks later, a bottle of Diet Dr Pepper arrived in Steinberg's office, except this one had a picture of the applicant in place of the logo. The ingredients listed on this doctored bottle said things like "100 percent perseverance" and "100 percent work ethic" and gave the product's establishment date as 1995 (presumably the applicant's birth year) rather than 1888.

Steinberg hired both.

7

Becoming a Sports Agent

Former agent Josh Luchs recalled the first time he paid a player. He likened it to a first kiss. "For me, the first time I broke an NCAA rule to try to land a client is just as indelible," Luchs explained in a confessional he wrote for *Sports Illustrated* in 2010, a few years after a suspension caused him to leave the profession. He had flown to Colorado to introduce himself to an oversize linebacker the world was convinced would go high in the draft once his college playing days were over. Thirty minutes into the conversation, the guy hit him up for $2,500.

Luchs gave the linebacker his money. He would pay two more collegians that year, but none of them chose him as their agent—which led to his first big lesson: handing a prospect a brick of bills was no way to build a long-term relationship. Instead, he decided he would give a player a few hundred dollars a month to ensure that they stayed in regular touch. He bought them meals and concert tickets and paid for hotel rooms, and even bailed one prospect out of jail—knowing all the time that each instance was a clear violation of NCAA rules. He told himself that the schools and the NCAA were making all this money while the players, many of them from poor families, were struggling. Besides, others were doing it. "I knew that if they didn't take our money," he said, "they would take it from one of the dozens of other agents opening their wallets."

The reality for any aspiring agent is that the competition doesn't always play fair. The NCAA has its rules, as do the various Players Associations, and states have enacted stricter laws to better regulate agents, yet bribes and fraud remain a part of the arsenal of unscrupulous agents looking for an in. "If someone chooses to be in this business," said Matt Sosnick, "they just have to recognize that the lying and the rest of the underhanded stuff is a part of it."

"We don't operate like that," said Rafa Nieves at Wasserman, which is second only to CAA in terms of contracts under management ($4.2 billion) and commissions generated ($209 million). "We have too much to lose. We have integrity. But there are people out there [who] don't want to put in the time or the hard work. They say, 'Let me take a shortcut to success.' You have to live with that."

The profession is disproportionately white, even in sports like basketball and football, where the players are disproportionately black. It's also overwhelmingly male. "Women Make Gains in NFL Agent Business" was the headline above a 2017 article Liz Mullen wrote for the *Sports Business Journal*. At that point, forty-one of the league's certified agents were women, more than half of whom represented at least one player. Two years later, Mullen asked the NFL Players Associations to run the numbers again. "There was a *drop* in women," she said. Seven fewer women were working as certified agents, and only seventeen actually represented a client.

"The whole business is extremely male-dominated, and of course predominantly white," said Nancy Lough, a sports marketing professor at UNLV and president of the Sport Marketing Association. But Lough finds reason for optimism in the students of all races and genders who tell her they want to be sports agents, even if she's not sure that's a good thing. Sure, it would be great to shift the industry's power imbalance, but she worries that for many, the idea of being an agent is based in fantasy. "I think for a lot, it's this idea of getting in with one of these young athletes they watched while in college and living that life," Lough said. "There are a lot of people who think they want to be an agent, but I don't think most know what that even means."

Lough's advice to students interested in becoming agents is to go to law school. "The truth is, if you have a client, you can be an agent," she said. "But if you want to do it right, you become a lawyer first."

Yet plenty of successful agents have no law degree. Rafa Nieves was a Venezuelan kid who was practically stranded in America when, at age nineteen, he flamed out after stints with the Detroit Tigers and the New York Yankees. There were several years lost to drinking when he was making a ton of money promoting clubs in Miami, but, once he was clean and sober, he talked his way into an internship with a large, established agency. He stuck with his day job—which in his case kept him out until two or three in the morning—and spent his afternoons and early evenings searching for recruits. He hung around spring training facilities when the pro teams were in town, and then, once the regular season started, went looking for prospects among the two big minor leagues in the area (the Gulf Coast League and the Florida State League). He had no luck with the white or black players but signed one or two out of every three Latino players he met. "I said screw the Americans, I'll just focus on the Latino guys," Nieves said. He hasn't been in the business for even a decade, yet he already represents a long list of major leaguers, including White Sox closer Alex Colomé, who will be paid $10.3 million in 2020, and Colomé's teammate Kelvin Herrera, an All-Star pitcher who'll collect $8.5 million.

"I don't need to be a lawyer," Nieves said. "I have five lawyers in my office. If I have to draft a contract or need someone to look over a contract, that's what they're there for. If there's something that needs to be changed, they tell me, and I deal with it." Early on, he loved competing with the lawyer-agents pursuing the same players he was. "[The players] would totally click with me, which was different from sitting with a guy who had never played baseball, he's just a lawyer," he said.

More important than any credential, Nieves said, is to act ethically: "A good friend of mine, a financial adviser, told me when I started in the business, 'You don't need to be the best agent in baseball to be successful. You just need to be the one that lasts the longest.' I didn't understand that until a year or two later, when I started seeing people who were my direct competitors falling like flies because they all tried to cut corners." One of them represented Melky Cabrera. Cabrera was the MVP of baseball's 2012 All-Star Game and then, one month later, was caught using a performance-enhancing drug and was suspended for fifty games. "He [the agent] fabricated a website to help Melky cover it up and got caught," Nieves said of his friend. "The guy was doing great. He had Cabrera, Nelson Cruz [a six-time All Star]. That guy could be making millions today. But he jeopardized his career over something like that." Over the years, three of Nieves's clients have been suspended for using performance-enhancing drugs. "I told them, 'I'll help you deal with it, but I'm not going to lie to get you out of it.' I'm not putting myself in a position so we both go down."

Leigh Steinberg is a lawyer but doesn't recommend law school. "Study business," he suggested. He's seen it again and again, he said: liberal-arts majors wanting in to the industry but for whom "business isn't natural." Gaining a "master's in caponomics," as he put it, requires a facility for numbers, not legal knowledge. "You need to study business as much as possible so you get basic business concepts," he suggested.

An innate sense of business has aided Matt Sosnick, another nonlawyer who has carved out a successful living as a baseball agent. It was the money Sosnick made helping to run a family business in his twenties that let him survive the dozen or so years it took for him to succeed as an agent. Sosnick would exit the business at the end of 2019 after an arrest on charges of domestic violence, and his firm would rename itself Apex Baseball. By that time, the agency he had cofounded two decades earlier represented more than fifty major leaguers, including Blake Snell, who won the American League Cy Young Award in 2018 (his reward was a five-year, $50 million contract), and Max Kepler, who in 2019 signed a five-year, $35 million contract extension with the Minnesota Twins.

Sosnick was still a working agent when I asked him what advice he'd give to anyone thinking of entering the profession. "Become a financial adviser instead," he said. "You can take care of a person's money for fifty years. You can make a commission on people's money for fifty years, rather than for six years. And it's a lot less competitive." And if you still insist on trying to break into the field? "You have to be a Type A and outgoing and aggressive," he said. "And you not only need to be aggressive, you have to be aggressively likable. And that's pretty tough to do sometimes."

Some blame sports agents for ruining football and other sports. There's no doubt the NFL, like virtually every sport, has been perverted by money. The salaries are mind-boggling and the ticket prices obscene, but the agent plays the role of the great equalizer. NFL franchises receive a honeypot of $250 million a year in television dollars. Shouldn't it be the players—the highly skilled beings who put their bodies on the line for our entertainment—who enjoy the greatest share of that money? A salary cap of $188.2 million in 2019 means that those on the field receive roughly three-quarters of the television dollars, leaving a 25 percent share for the owners (or more; there were nine NFL teams that were at least $20 million under the cap at the end of the 2019 season)— and add to that all the money franchises earn on tickets, corporate suites, concessions, sponsorships and other deals. The NFL was a $14 billion behemoth in 2019, with each franchise making, on average, around $100 million in profit every year. It's still the owners who are the biggest financial winners at the end of each season.

There's always worry about the future of football. Concerns over concussions and degenerative brain injuries have led to a drop of more than 20 percent in the number of young people playing tackle football. The league has become a flash point in the culture wars, which has led, at least temporarily, to a drop in viewership and attendance. Yet that, too, seems like it should be of little concern to an aspiring football agent, given all the new records the sport continues to establish. Football is only growing. Advertisers spent a record $4.6 billion on commercials during NFL games in 2017, despite legitimate concerns about players' health and all the political fireworks around the game. That year, thirty-seven of the top fifty broadcasts in terms of viewership on US television were NFL games, *Bloomberg Business-Week* reported, including four of the top five. The league's share of playoff advertising dollars relative to its big three competitors in the United States—the NBA, Major League Baseball, and the National Hockey League—increased from 52 percent to 62 percent in just four years. The average NFL franchise was worth $2.9 billion in 2019, according to *Forbes*. The Dallas Cowboys were valued at $5.5 billion, the New York Giants at $3.9 billion, and the Los Angeles Rams at $3.8 billion. The future of the game appears to be secure.

Every sport seems to have its share of bad off-the-field behavior. For some, that might be a reason to reconsider the dream of becoming a sports agent. As Josh Luchs asked in his *Sports Illustrated* confessional, "When [his client was] thrown in jail for shooting off a gun . . . whom do you think he called in the middle of the night to bail him out?" On that front, some agents are busier than others. Brian Murphy, the younger agent who, along with David Dunn, took half of Steinberg's clients at the start of the 2000s, represented Aaron Hernandez, the New England Patriots tight end who was convicted of murder, and Dunn represented Richie Incognito, the white player the Miami Dolphins suspended in 2013 after hearing a voice mail he left for a teammate calling him a "half-nig**r piece of shit" and threatening to slap his mother across the face. Another offshoot of Steinberg's firm, Rep1 Sports, represented Ray Lewis, who pled guilty to obstruction of justice after he admitted that he lied to the police about a fight in Atlanta in January of 2000 that left two men dead. A Fulton County Superior Court judge sentenced Lewis to twelve months' probation, and the NFL hit him with a $250,000 fine.

Yet on that front, no agent seemed as busy as Drew Rosenhaus. One of his University of Miami recruits, Brian Blades, was convicted of manslaughter (a ruling the trial judge reversed a few days later) and, as *Sports Illustrated* reported, "Rosenhaus was right there, fielding questions from journalists, comforting Blades's family, cheering on his lawyers."

Plaxico Burress, the star receiver Rosenhaus signed after Steinberg's great fall, kept his agent equally busy during the 2008 season, when there were two domestic disturbance calls to Burress's home, followed by his accidentally shooting himself in the leg in a New York City nightclub. The Giants suspended him for the rest of the season and withheld his pay for those final four games. An arbitrator, however, ordered the team to send Burress the $1 million the team owed him. Presumably, Rosenhaus received his full commission.

The same probably won't be said of Rosenhaus's highest-profile player of the 2019 season, Antonio Brown. Rosenhaus had done well by his client when he secured a three-year, $50.1 million deal with the Oakland Raiders—but the Raiders voided the contract before the season started after a series of events that included Brown's very public feud with the league over his helmet and then an even louder, nastier fight with the team's GM. There were, no doubt, plenty of late-night calls between Rosenhaus and his client as all that was taking place, and then more concerning the two-year, $15 million deal Rosenhaus was able to negotiate with the Patriots. But Brown was let go by the Pats after one game, and, depending on the week, wanted nothing more to do with football or was desperate to play again. As of December 2019, the Raiders had paid Brown $1.2 million, according to Spotrac.com, which tracks contracts in the NFL and other leagues, and the Patriots had paid him all of $154,000. If an agent's job includes curbing a client's worst instincts, Rosenhaus had failed miserably, and it cost him. Assuming that Rosenhaus charged the customary 3 percent (rivals have complained that he sometimes cuts his rate to lure away a client), his inability to keep Brown in check was the difference between the $36,000 in fees he would have already received and the $1.5 million he could have made. In January, Rosenhaus conditionally terminated his relationship with Brown until the receiver sought counseling.

Increasingly, agents in every sport are having to help clients handle everything from domestic violence charges to failed drug tests to high-profile embarrassments. "You never stop being there to help them with the off-field stuff," Rafa Nieves said. "That's what this job is. It's all about relationships and customer care. Care about your customers, your clients. Go above and beyond for them"—and that way they'll have no reason to start looking for another agent.

And yet clients do leave, even when an agent feels that he or she has gone well beyond the norm. They've invested all of themselves in a client, but a Scott Boras in baseball or a

Drew Rosenhaus in football lures them away with promises of a richer payday. "Sometimes I look around this business and wonder why anyone wants to become an agent," Matt Sosnick said. Like so many agents, however, he's only talk. That night he was flying to Tampa Bay to see three of his players, including his $10-million-a-year Cy Young winner, Blake Snell. "It's also a great life, and I feel fortunate every day I'm doing it."

ACKNOWLEDGMENTS

First, my heartfelt gratitude to all those who agreed to talk with me for this book. I had been forewarned: sports agents, as a group, are not inclined to open up to those outside the fraternity. Thank you to Tory, Leigh, Don, Rafa, and Matt for generously giving of your time and of yourselves. Thanks as well to Beth McClinton at CAA, who connected me with Tory. And thanks to the assist provided by Ethan Hausser in helping to make parts of this book possible.

As always, thanks to my own superagent, Elizabeth Kaplan. I'm obliged to Simon & Schuster's Jonathan Karp and Ben Loehnen for inviting me to be part of the Masters at Work series, and also to Stuart Roberts, who proved a master at work when editing this manuscript. Thanks as well to Benjamin Holmes for the care with which he copyedited this book, saving me from myself and silly mistakes time and again. A big shout-out as well to friend and former colleague Ken Belson, who covers football for the *New York Times*. It was Ken who connected me with the incomparable Don Yee and offered advice and guidance along the way.

And finally, my family. Gratitude and love to Daisy Walker and our two boys, Oliver and Silas, who never seemed so impressed with their old man as when he told them he had just had breakfast with Tom Brady's agent or spent an afternoon with the agent for Patrick Mahomes. This book is for the three of you.

APPENDIX:
PRACTICAL ADVICE

Bob Boland, the former football agent turned academic, helped create a graduate program in sports management at NYU. He taught there for fourteen years before taking over the MBA/Master's in Sports Administration program at Ohio University, which is considered one of the country's more prestigious graduate sports business programs. Since 2017, Boland has worked at Penn State University, where he holds the unusual title of athletics integrity officer. He knows a great deal about sports and the law and sports management generally. Yet the question he's most often asked by undergraduates: How do I become a sports agent?

"I used to tell students, 'If you represented Nike and did all the deals for Nike with the players, except you're not collecting a commission from a player but a salary for representing the company, would you consider yourself a failure?'" Boland said. Students always answered no, because of course a job at Nike negotiating with an agent on some deal would be a dream job.

And then invariably the student, ignoring the point, would press ahead, looking for tips on making it as a sports agent.

Virtually every agent I spoke with recommended learning the CBA—the collective bargaining agreement—that every league has worked out between the owners and players. The CBAs lay out the nuances of salary caps and the rights granted to players and their representatives. In March 2020, the NFL and the Players Association hammered out a new CBA that extends through the end of the 2030 season and gives the owners the option to expand the regular season from sixteen games to seventeen games as early as 2021. "Learn that CBA like it's your bible," said one agent who preferred that I not use his name.

Leigh Steinberg has his Sports Career Conferences and his Agent Academy, which hold seminars in cities around the country. There, for a few hundred dollars, attendees can hear from Steinberg directly, along with the panels of team executives, social media managers, and beat reporters Steinberg and his people assemble. He touts the events as perfect introductions for anyone interested in breaking into the industry, but more than one person I spoke with looked skeptically on this side venture.

Read the *Sports Agent Blog* (http://sportsagentblog.com/), written by Darren Heitner, and follow him on Twitter (@Sports AgentBlog). Heitner is a lawyer who has authored two sports law books and writes for both *Forbes* and *Inc.* Buying a subscription to Liz Mullen's *Sports Business Daily* would cost more than $300 a year, but many of her articles aren't blocked by the paywall. Check out websites such as Spotrac.com, which tracks player salaries in a wide range of sports.

Everyone (well, everyone but Sosnick) recommended an internship as a way into the industry. "Go work for an agent, whatever the job is, even if you've got to make coffee for the first three months," said Jason Belzer, who decided he wanted to be an agent while an undergrad enrolled in the sports management program at Rutgers University. Working as an intern lets you know if the business is really right for you, he said, but, more important, "you'll [have] a significant advantage if you can get in the door somewhere and work your way up."

Belzer landed an internship at an established agency in New York City that represented news and sports broadcasters, and he also worked with a couple of retired coaches. Next he interned for an agency in Virginia that represented professional athletes. "I quickly realized that I didn't want to work with athletes, because I learned it was very much like babysitting," said Belzer, now thirty-three. "You're spending all your time trying to convince seventeen- and eighteen-year-olds to sign with you." After earning an MBA at the University of Illinois and returning to Rutgers for law school, he carved out a niche representing college coaches. By 2019, he was representing forty head coaches and another thirty-five or so assistant coaches. That included basketball coach Chris Holtmann, who signed an eight-year, $26 million contract with Ohio State University in 2018.

"If all goes well, Coach Holtmann will be staying for the next thirty years," Belzer said. That's one advantage of a practice centered on coaches: a longevity that isn't possible with elite athletes. Coaches are also less inclined to jump from agent to agent, said Belzer, who writes a popular sports business blog at Forbes.com and also teaches in the sports management program at Rutgers that first exposed him to the business. Find your niche, he advised. As an example, he mentioned someone he had met a couple of weeks earlier who'd spent a year in Europe building relationships with European basketball teams.

"He's getting guys jobs in the NBA," he said, even if so far his clients have been benchwarmers. "He understands that he has to build a book of business versus thinking he can convince some big prospect to sign with him when he has no track record."

Rafa Nieves is another big proponent of internships. Like Belzer, he sees an internship as a chance to try on the occupation before fully committing to it. "You're never going to know if it's for you unless you get out into the field and do it," he said.

"I've seen agents come in, they get two or three clients, and then, after all that work, they say, 'Screw this, I don't like this, this is not for me, this isn't what I thought it would be.'"

But Nieves also had a warning: don't expect to get paid, at least at first. "We have people apply to Wasserman, they interview well, and we'd like to give them a shot, but they ask, 'How much are you going to pay me?'" he said. The problem is that they arrive having almost no practical skills that would justify a salary. "They need help figuring out how to rent a car from Hertz," he said. "They don't know the first thing about taxes, they don't know the CBA. They don't know anything."

Over breakfast, Nieves recounted the conversations he's had with prospective interns who refuse to work unless they're paid. "They'll say, 'Oh, but I have a college degree,'" he said. "So what? I've never met with an athlete ever, and I'm sure no [other] NBA or NFL agent has met with an athlete, who asked, 'Where did you go to college? Do you have a law degree?' An athlete is going to ask you who you've represented, how you're going to help [their] career and make [them] more money, and how are you better than others." Nieves earned no salary as an intern during his first months on the job—only a $1,000 bonus for every player he signed. The full-time recruiting position he was offered in January 2012 paid a salary of maybe $30,000 a year, along with the same $1,000-per-player bonus. "I probably made $50,000 that year," he said.

There's no better way for a junior employee, paid or unpaid, to impress the agent who has hired him or her than recruiting players. Proximity often dictates success. In his first several years helping Eugene Parker and Roosevelt Barnes with recruiting, Tory Dandy focused primarily on South Carolina. "It was less expensive than flying around the US and paying for cars and hotels," Dandy said. Drew Rosenhaus built his practice by recruiting at his alma mater, the University of Miami. Don Yee focused on smaller schools within driving distance early in his practice—colleges where he also knew there would be less competition for talented players. Get to know the coaches there. Attend the games, and really get invested in the program. Signing one player at a school makes it much easier to land future talent there. Dandy branched out beyond schools he could reach by car and recruited first one player at Temple University and then two more. The same thing happened at Clemson University, the alma mater of four of his clients he signed in 2019. Dandy signed Marshon Lattimore, a talented Ohio State cornerback the Saints chose with the eleventh pick of the 2017 draft, and in 2018 he represented Denzel Ward, another talented cornerback from Ohio State, whom the Browns chose fourth overall that year. Together, Lattimore and Ward alone represented $44 million in contracts and generated $1.3 million in fees.

And, finally, there's Boland's bigger point: there are plenty of interesting jobs in the wider world of player representation. "Being a sports agent is sort of an accidental career," he said. "You can move in that direction, but you're not going to have any success unless you have clients." There are plenty of ways to be part of the sports-agent world short of certification. CAA, for instance, employs more than six hundred people in its sports division, and only a tiny fraction of them are certified agents.

"I think a lot of people miss the idea that there are a lot of jobs in the sports industry that use the skills that an agent learns: understanding negotiations, understanding contracts, understanding that there are all these skills that aren't representing an individual client but mean being involved in sports in the same way," Boland said. Maybe do data crunching for an agency, work in marketing or legal, or go to work in a GM's office and sit opposite a player's representative.

"Have a wider field of vision," Boland continued. "There are a lot of great jobs out there."

FURTHER READING

Below I recommend two works of journalism and an academic book for those seeking to read more about the fascinating world of sports agents, along with several memoirs that bring readers deeper into agents' murky and mysterious world.

Players: How Sports Became a Business, by Matthew Futterman (2016). Futterman, a sportswriter for the *Wall Street Journal*, offers an entertaining account of how sports grew into big business over the past half century. The first part of the book focuses mainly on Mark McCormack, widely considered the pioneer who created the profession, offering the origin story for anyone interested in learning more about the birth of the modern sports agent.

License to Deal: A Season on the Run with a Maverick Baseball Agent, by Jerry Crasnick (2005). Crasnick, who covered the business of sports first for Bloomberg and then for ESPN, spent a year chronicling the life and struggles of baseball agent Matt Sosnick (quoted within these pages) long before anyone would have described him as one of the game's top agents. It's another good read that offers plenty of insight into the agent's life.

The Business of Sports Agents, Third Edition, by Kenneth L. Shropshire, Timothy Davis, and N. Jeremi Duru (2016). First published in 2003, this book has been a standard text used for years by sports management programs around the country. This third edition refreshes a work that takes a deeper dive into the history of the profession and its growth into a big business than is presented in these pages. It's also a good primer on the ethical and legal issues that any agent must consider.

The Agent: My 40-Year Career Making Deals and Changing the Game, by Leigh Steinberg with Michael Arkush (2014). Steinberg's version of his rise and fall is a readable account thick with war stories and lessons learned in his first four decades as an agent.

A Shark Never Sleeps: Wheeling and Dealing with the NFL's Most Ruthless Agent, by Drew Rosenhaus with Don Yaeger and Jason Rosenhaus (1997). This is a hot mess of a memoir; the text is repetitive, and Rosenhaus proves the most grating of narrators. But between boasts, he offers helpful advice and also reminds readers that getting to the top requires hard work and dedication.

My Brother's Keeper: Above & Beyond "The Dotted Line" with the NFL's Most Ethical Agent, by Eugene Lee (2015). Lee was featured in Morgan Spurlock's engaging 2011 documentary about sports agents, *The Dotted Line*, and parlayed that bit of fame into a memoir that brings readers on the road with him as he vies for clients. I'm not sure he's the NFL's most ethical agent, as his book's subtitle claims, but this is an honest account of making it in a tough profession.

The Power of Nice: How to Negotiate So Everyone Wins— Especially You!, by Ronald M. Shapiro and Mark A. Jankowski with James Dale (1998). Longtime baseball agent Ron Shapiro takes you through what he calls the "three Ps" of negotiating— prepare, probe, and propose—in a book filled with anecdotes and insights.

ABOUT THE AUTHOR

Gary Rivlin is a Pulitzer Prize–winning investigative reporter and the author of six books, including *Katrina: After the Flood*. His work has appeared in the *New York Times Magazine*, *Mother Jones*, *GQ*, and *Wired*, among other publications. He is a two-time Gerald Loeb Award winner and a former reporter for the *New York Times*. He lives in New York with his wife, theater director Daisy Walker, and two sons.